SENSELESS SENSIBILITIES

CREATE YOUR OWN AUSTEN-TATIOUS MASH-UP!

This most beloved work belongs to

_____

Cover and interior design by Danielle Deschenes
Text by Patrick Baker

Passages "Checking In at the Ritz-Mansfield," "Mansfield-Gate," and
"Celebs with Benefits" by Kitty Raymond

www.clarksonpotter.com
ISBN 978-0-307-88642-2
Printed in China

Dear Reader,

WHEN MY AGENTS CALLED me up to tell me about this job, I was ecstatic. The idea of thrilled me, because I would get paid for it. Premium cable isn't cheap, and there's no way Mama's missing *Weeds*, you know? My agent told me that this publisher was looking for a modern Jane Austen adaptation. Kate Gosselin was busy and the cast of *Jersey Shore* didn't seem to want the job, so I was their woman!

When I brought in my idea for a Latino version of *Sense and Sensibility*, my editor told me that *From Prada to Nada* was already filming. When I wrote an outline for *Emma* set at a Beverly Hills high school, she told me that *Clueless* was made fifteen years ago. When I brought them my manuscript for a loose adaptation of *Pride and Prejudice* in diary form, I was informed that I had just handed in a copy of *Bridget Jones's Diary*, and that the publisher was beginning to regret not pushing harder for Kate. Frustrated that I couldn't please the unpleasable, I snidely said I should just take half of Jane Austen's words and leave the rest blank for my readers to fill in themselves. To my surprise, my editor agreed to this. It was mainly to get me out of her office, I think, but what does it matter as long as *Dexter* stays on my television?

A quick note about how to enjoy this book: I strongly recommend you play with others, but if you're a shut-in or a hoarder or some other socially inept human like I see on TLC, then I guess you can play by yourself. All you have to do is fill in the blanks, and then plug what you wrote into the passage on the next page. Also, don't look at the passage beforehand, cheater.

Enjoy the book, share it with your friends, but be sure to make them buy their own copy, OK? I'm not missing *True Blood* because your friends are cheap.

Sincerely,

Ima Hack

HEY, EVERYONE!
LET'S MESS WITH A UNIVERSALLY ACKNOWLEDGED TRUTH!

The opening lines of *Pride and Prejudice* are so well known, so often quoted, so revered, that I never, ever want to hear them uttered again. It's like hearing someone say "Where's the beef?" or "That's what *she* said" and expecting you to laugh like you did in 1992. Change this up a bit for the good of all of us. (Just this once, you can go ahead and peek at the passage for inspiration.)

NOUN	1	Ellie Yacauno
NOUN	2	Palisades mall
NOUN	3	Barbie
THE NOUN FROM #1	4	Ellie Yacauno
YOUR NEIGHBORHOOD	5	Washington Twp.
PEOPLE IN YOUR NEIGHBORHOOD	6	The adams Family
AN OCCUPATION	7	anthropologist

It is a truth universally acknowledged, that a single 1 *Ellie Yacovino*
in possession of a good 2 *Palisades mall* must be in want of a[n]
3 *Barbie*.

However little known the feelings or views of such a[n]
4 *Ellie Yacovino* may be on his first entering
5 *Washington Twp.*, this truth is so well fixed in the minds of the
surrounding 6 *adams Family*, that he is considered as the
rightful 7 *anthropologists* of some one or other of their daughters.

SIMPLY SHOCKING!!

EVERYTHING
TO EVERYONE

I n *Pride and Prejudice*, Darcy has some pretty big demands for what he wants in a lady friend. If Darcy were a modern man, he'd be looking for a woman who knows her way around the bedroom, kitchen, home office, bedroom, ballroom, study, bedroom, dining room, nursery, and of course . . . bedroom. In short, Darcy wants what every man wants in a woman: all of it. Fill in the blanks to hear some more of Darcy's ridiculous demands.

SLANG FOR "A LOT"	1	_____
MORE SLANG FOR "A LOT"	2	_____
SYNONYM OR SLANG FOR "ATTRACTIVE"	3	_____
A SUBJECT OF STUDY	4	_____
A SKILL	5	_____
ANOTHER SKILL	6	_____
A SPORT	7	_____
NOUN (PLURAL)	8	_____
SYNONYM FOR "ESSENCE"	9	_____
VERB (ENDING IN –ING)	10	_____
A THING YOU OWN (PLURAL)	11	_____
ANOTHER THING YOU OWN (PLURAL)	12	_____
VERB (ENDING IN –ING)	13	_____

"Then," observed Elizabeth, "you must comprehend a[n] 1_____ in your idea of an accomplished woman."

"Yes; I do comprehend a[n] 2_____ in it."

"Oh! certainly," cried his faithful assistant, "no one can be really esteemed 3_____, who does not greatly surpass what is usually met with. A woman must have a thorough knowledge of 4_____, 5_____, 6_____, 7_____, and the modern 8_____, to deserve the word; and besides all this, she must possess a certain something in her 9_____ and manner of 10_____, the tone of her voice, her 11_____ and 12_____, or the word will be but half deserved."

"All this she must possess," added Darcy, "and to all this she must yet add something more substantial, in the improvement of her mind by extensive 13_____."

A-MALE-I-CAN
IDOL(IZE)

OK, ladies, now that we've discussed what men want, let's talk about what *you're* looking for in a partner. Good hair? A steady but interesting job? In-laws who don't require you to go to their house for the holidays? The ability to tear up but not weep over rom coms? Well, now's your chance! Fill in the blanks to get everything that you've ever wanted in a guy!*

*Offer on paper only

YOUR DREAM GUY	1	_____
SYNONYM FOR "WANTED"	2	_____
A QUALITY YOU WANT IN A GUY	3	_____
A QUALITY YOU WANT IN A GUY	4	_____
A QUALITY YOU WANT IN A GUY	5	_____
YOUR FAVORITE PARTS OF A MALE BODY	6	_____
A QUALITY YOU WANT IN A GUY	7	_____
A QUALITY YOU WANT IN A GUY	8	_____
SLANG FOR "GREAT"	9	_____
AN ACTIVITY YOU LOVE	10	_____

When Jane and Elizabeth were alone, the former, who had been cautious in her praise of 1_____ before, expressed to her sister how very much she 2_____ him.

"He is just what a young man ought to be," said she, "3_____, 4_____, 5_____; and I never saw such happy 6_____!—so much ease, with such perfect good 7_____!"

"He is also 8_____," replied Elizabeth, "which a young man ought likewise to be, if he possibly can. His character is thereby 9_____."

"I was very much flattered by his asking me to 10_____ a second time. I did not expect such a compliment."

TILL BS
DO US PART

Charlotte makes a very astute observation in *Pride and Prejudice* that a marriage's happiness is entirely a matter of chance, but we're not all Charlottes. And at every wedding, there's someone making predictions about whether or not the marriage will last. Usually this person is (a) not a marriage counselor, (b) in a couple of marriages deep themselves, (c) in more than a couple of drinks deep, or (d) all of the above. Fill in the blanks to hear some of the worst marriage advice ever.

A PERSON WHO GIVES BAD ADVICE	**1**	_____
SOMEONE YOU KNOW WHO WOULD BE A BAD CHOICE FOR A HUSBAND	**2**	_____
A BODY PART	**3**	_____
A NUMBER	**4**	_____
NOUN (PLURAL)	**5**	_____
THE NOUN FROM #5	**6**	_____
ADJECTIVE	**7**	_____
ADJECTIVE	**8**	_____
A STATE OF BEING (EXAMPLE: HAPPINESS, SADNESS, ANGER, ETC.)	**9**	_____
ADJECTIVE	**10**	_____
ANOTHER STATE OF BEING	**11**	_____
NOUN (PLURAL)	**12**	_____

"Well," said **1**_____, "I wish Jane success with all my heart; and if she were married to **2**_____ to-morrow, I should think she had as good a chance of happiness as if she were to be studying his **3**_____ for a[n] **4**_____ month. Happiness in marriage is entirely a matter of **5**_____. If the **6**_____ of the parties are ever so **7**_____ to each other, or ever so **8**_____ before-hand, it does not advance their **9**_____ in the least. They always contrive to grow sufficiently **10**_____ afterwards to have their share of **11**_____; and it is better to know as little as possible of the **12**_____ of the person with whom you are to pass your life."

BROS BEFORE
PITIABLE WOMEN

I n *Pride and Prejudice*, Lady Catherine tells Elizabeth that she should not expect recognition, or even well wishes, from Darcy's family if she marries him. And it's true; you gotta get on the good side of a guy's family. Only these days, the guy's family extends to his college friends, his drinking buddies from work, his fantasy football league, and his Southern-rock cover band. Fill in the blanks to see Lady Catherine warning Elizabeth against bromancing the bro-mafia.

A CLUB OR ORGANIZATION MEN JOIN	1	_____
ANOTHER CLUB OR ORGANIZATION FOR MEN	2	_____
SLANG FOR "MALE FRIENDS"	3	_____
AN ACTIVITY MEN LIKE	4	_____
ANOTHER ACTIVITY MEN LIKE	5	_____
ANOTHER ACTIVITY MEN LIKE	6	_____
ANOTHER ACTIVITY MEN LIKE	7	_____
THE ACTIVITY FROM #7	8	_____
A GROUP OF PEOPLE A GUY MIGHT HANG WITH	9	_____
ANOTHER GROUP A GUY MIGHT HANG WITH	10	_____
NEGATIVE VERB (PAST TENSE)	11	_____
ANOTHER NEGATIVE VERB (PAST TENSE)	12	_____
ANOTHER NEGATIVE VERB (PAST TENSE)	13	_____

"If Mr. Darcy is neither by 1_____ nor 2_____ confined to his 3_____, why is not he to make another choice? And if I am that choice, why may not I accept him?"

"Because 4_____, 5_____, 6_____, nay, 7_____, forbid it. Yes, Miss Bennet, 8_____; for do not expect to be noticed by his 9_____ or 10_____, if you willfully act against the inclinations of all. You will be 11_____, 12_____, and 13_____, by every one connected with him."

OUTRAGEOUS!

BAD-NEWS
BEAU

I n *Pride and Prejudice*, Wickham is bad news for Kitty. "Bad news" can mean lots of things. It can mean he's just not your kind of guy, or that he's an opposing personality type, or that you want different things, or that he's wanted in five states for drug running and for sleeping with the chief of Interpol's daughter, then robbing her. In this case, "bad news" means the latter. Fill in the blanks to meet Kitty's bad-to-the-bone boyfriend.

AN ILLICIT PROFESSION	1	_____
SLANG FOR "CHARM" (EXAMPLE: MOJO, VIBE, AURA, ETC.)	2	_____
SLANG FOR "GREAT"	3	_____
ANOTHER ILLICIT PROFESSION	4	_____
A FEMALE FAMILY MEMBER	5	_____
A NEIGHBORHOOD YOU DON'T WANT TO VISIT	6	_____
A BODY PART	7	_____
ADJECTIVE	8	_____
ADJECTIVE	9	_____
ADJECTIVE	10	_____
A TERRIBLE PLACE TO RUN AWAY TO	11	_____

He was declared to be in debt to every 1_____ in the place, and his 2_____, all honored with the title of 3_____, had been extended into every 4_____'s 5_____. Every body declared that he was the wickedest young man in 6_____; and every body began to find out that they had always distrusted the appearance of his 7_____. Elizabeth, though she did not credit above half of what was said, believed enough to make her 8_____ assurance of her sister's ruin still more 9_____; and even Jane, who believed still less of it, became almost 10_____, more especially as the time was now come when, if they had gone to 11_____, which she had never before entirely despaired of, they must in all probability have gained some news of them.

WILL YOU
(PLEASE NEVER, EVER) MARRY ME?

I t's the dream of every little girl. To be taken to the top of the hill on a moon-lit evening by your beloved. Then, as the city lights shimmer before you, he gets down on one knee, pulls a ring from his pocket, and proceeds to insult you and your family, making the world's worst proposal. And your answer, without a doubt, is "What? Marry you . . . why would I . . . just take me back to the car! Ugh!" You don't think it'll happen that way, but it can. Just ask Elizabeth from *Pride and Prejudice*. Fill in the blanks to hear the kind of proposal you just can't say yes to.

A CRAPPY LOCATION	1	_____
VERB (PAST TENSE)	2	_____
VERB (PAST TENSE)	3	_____
ADVERB	4	_____
VERB	5	_____
VERB (PAST TENSE)	6	_____
VERB (PAST TENSE)	7	_____
VERB (PAST TENSE)	8	_____
ADJECTIVE	9	_____
ADVERB	10	_____
NEGATIVE ADJECTIVE	11	_____
A BODY PART	12	_____
SLANG FOR "SEX"	13	_____

"In 1_____ have I 2_____. It will not do. My feelings will not be 3_____. You must allow me to tell you how 4_____ I 5_____ and love you."

Elizabeth's astonishment was beyond expression. She 6_____, 7_____, 8_____, and was silent. This he considered 9_____ encouragement, and the avowal of all that he felt and had long felt for her 10_____ followed. He spoke 11_____, but there were feelings besides those of the 12_____ to be detailed, and he was not more eloquent on the subject of tenderness than of 13_____.

SIMPLY SHOCKING!!

NONSENSE
AND INSENSIBILITY

Pride and Prejudice's Mr. Collins is, as is plainly stated in the text, not a sensible man. Now, that may have flown when Jane wrote the book (it was the Enlightenment, after all), but for modern readers, it might not cut the cake. In an age where politicians go on reality shows, where people use the Internet to broadcast what they're having for lunch, and where there's a gourmet dog-biscuit shop around the corner called the Bakery for Dogs, the benchmark for "sensible" has gone down a few notches. So, to make Mr. Collins truly insensible for a modern audience, fill in the blanks.

NOUN (PLURAL)	1	_____
ANOTHER NOUN (PLURAL)	2	_____
ADJECTIVE	3	_____
ADJECTIVE	4	_____
AN OCCUPATION	5	_____
A CLUB (EXAMPLE: CHESS CLUB, THE KNIGHTS OF COLUMBUS, ETC.)	6	_____
AN ITEM THIS CLUB WOULD USE	7	_____
VERB (ENDING IN -ING)	8	_____
NONGEOGRAPHICAL LOCATION (PLURAL) (EXAMPLE: GAS STATIONS, POST OFFICES, ETC.)	9	_____
THE OCCUPATION FROM #5	10	_____
A BODY PART (PLURAL)	11	_____
A STATE OF BEING (EXAMPLE: HAPPINESS, SADNESS, ANGER, ETC.)	12	_____
A BODY PART	13	_____
A CITY YOU HATE	14	_____
NOUN (PLURAL)	15	_____

Mr. Collins was not a sensible man, and the deficiency of nature had been but little assisted by 1_____ or 2_____; the greatest part of his life having been spent under the guidance of a[n] 3_____ and 4_____ 5_____; and though he belonged to one of the 6_____, he had merely kept the 7_____, without 8_____ at it any 9_____. The subjection in which his 10_____ had brought him up had given him originally great 11_____, but it was now a good deal counteracted by the 12_____ of a weak 13_____, living in 14_____, and the consequential feelings of early and unexpected 15_____.

CHECKING IN
AT THE RITZ-MANSFIELD

Hell hath no fury like a diva who gets anything less than four-star treatment. We all know what happens when an A-lister discovers she's booked at a B-level hotel: One minute she's frozen in the doorway, the next minute some hapless personal assistant gets clocked in the noggin with a Swarovski-crystal-encrusted cell phone. Now imagine if Goody Two-Shoes Fanny from *Mansfield Park* is actually Paris Hilton's new BFF.

SYNONYM FOR "TACKY"   **1**   _____

AN ILLICIT ACTIVITY THAT MIGHT HAPPEN AT A HOLLYWOOD PARTY   **2**   _____

SYNONYM FOR "TACKY"   **3**   _____

A CHEAP MATERIAL   **4**   _____

SOMETHING YOU WOULD FIND IN A HOTEL ROOM   **5**   _____

A MALE CELEBRITY   **6**   _____

THE NAME OF A FANCY HOTEL   **7**   _____

SYNONYM FOR "EXPENSIVE"   **8**   _____

SYNONYM FOR "FANCY"   **9**   _____

ANOTHER SYNONYM FOR "FANCY"   **10**   _____

A SMALL LUXURY ITEM (PLURAL)   **11**   _____

ANOTHER SMALL LUXURY ITEM (PLURAL)   **12**   _____

AN AMENITY YOU'D FIND AT A FANCY RESORT (PLURAL) (EXAMPLE: SPAS, MASSEUSES, ETC.)   **13**   _____

A TYPE OF EMPLOYEE A CELEB WOULD HAVE (PLURAL) (EXAMPLE: BODYGUARDS, MANICURISTS, ETC.)   **14**   _____

ANOTHER TYPE OF EMPLOYEE A CELEB WOULD HAVE (PLURAL)   **15**   _____

A TERM FOR A LOW-LEVEL EMPLOYEE (PLURAL)   **16**   _____

PHRASE MEANING "YELL AT"   **17**   _____

A TYPE OF PERSON THAT WOULD BE CONSIDERED A VIP (EXAMPLE: A MOVIE STAR, A CELEBRITY, ETC.)   **18**   _____

SYNONYM FOR "PEACEFULLY" OR "HAPPILY"   **19**   _____

Fanny's imagination had prepared her for something grander than a mere 1_____, oblong room, fitted up for the purpose of 2_____—with nothing more striking or more 3_____ than the profusion of 4_____, and the crimson velvet cushions appearing over the 5_____.

"I am disappointed," said she, in a low voice to 6_____.

"This is not my idea of a 7_____. There is nothing 8_____ here, nothing 9_____, nothing 10_____. Here are no 11_____, no 12_____, no 13_____, no 14_____. No 15_____, 16_____ to 17_____. No signs that a[n] 18_____ sleeps 19_____."

UNIVERSAL STUDIOS
THEME ~~MANSFIELD~~ PARK

Mary Crawford, of *Mansfield Park* fame, doesn't think too highly of clergymen. She finds them to be lousy do-nothings for whom a hard day's work probably includes a mid-afternoon nap. And while the clergy do have some PR problems (we're looking at you, Flying Nun), they don't have anything on the modern movie star. Should I go shopping on Rodeo Drive? Or bathe my Chihuahua in my Brentwood pool? Oh, the days are just packed! Fill in the blanks to hear Mary's tirade against the Hollywood It-Crowd.

A BAD MOVIE	1	_____
AN ITEM IN THE BAD MOVIE FROM #1	2	_____
THE NAME OF A THEATER, STAGE, OR STADIUM	3	_____
ANOTHER BAD MOVIE	4	_____
AN ITEM IN THE BAD MOVIE FROM #4	5	_____
A POSITIVE STATE OF BEING (LIKE HAPPINESS)	6	_____
ANOTHER STATE OF BEING	7	_____
A FILM-INDUSTRY JOB (NOT ACTOR)	8	_____
ANOTHER FILM-INDUSTRY JOB (NOT ACTOR)	9	_____
A TACKY LUXURY ITEM	10	_____
SOMETHING A MOVIE STAR MIGHT DO	11	_____
SOMETHING ELSE A MOVIE STAR MIGHT DO	12	_____
ADJECTIVE TO DESCRIBE A MOVIE STAR	13	_____
SYNONYM FOR "MOVIE STAR"	14	_____
ADJECTIVE FOR A MOVIE STAR	15	_____
ANOTHER ADJECTIVE FOR A MOVIE STAR	16	_____
A TRASHY TABLOID	17	_____
A GOSSIPY TV SHOW	18	_____
SOMEONE WHO WORKS FOR AN ACTOR	19	_____
SOMEONE ELSE WHO WORKS FOR AN ACTOR	20	_____
UNFLATTERING VERB	21	_____

"What! Take 1_____ without a[n]

2_____! No, that is madness indeed; absolute madness."

"Shall I ask you how the 3_____ is to be filled, if a

man is neither to take 4_____ with a[n]

5_____, nor without? . . . As he cannot be influenced by

those feelings which you rank highly as 6_____ and

7_____ to the 8_____ and

9_____, in their choice of a profession, as heroism, and

noise, and fashion are all against him . . ."

"Oh, no doubt he is very sincere in preferring a[n]

10_____ ready made, to the trouble of working for one;

and has the best intentions of doing nothing all the rest of his days but

11_____, 12_____, and grow

13_____. . . . A 14_____ has nothing to

do but be 15_____ and 16_____—read

17_____, watch 18_____, and quarrel

with his 19_____. His 20_____ does all

the work, and the business of his own life is to 21_____."

THE BAD BOY
OF MANSFIELD PARK

Everyone's fallen for someone they know they shouldn't. For *Mansfield Park's* Fanny, it was Henry Crawford. For me, it was the guy who went to a pet shop to buy a puppy and ended up leaving with a snake. Then there was the guy who kept trying, and eventually succeeded, at guessing my e-mail password (I, for one, thought boomgoesthedynamite was a very secure password). But I digress. Surely you have a friend (and friend can mean you) who's had this happen to them. Fill in the blanks to hear her inner thoughts on the situation.

THE NAME OF YOUR FRIEND	1	_____
VERB (ENDING IN -ING)	2	_____
THE NAME OF THE GUY	3	_____
ADJECTIVE	4	_____
ADJECTIVE	5	_____
ADJECTIVE	6	_____
A HABIT THIS GUY HAS/HAD	7	_____
YOUR FRIEND'S JOB	8	_____
UNFLATTERING VERB (PAST TENSE)	9	_____
VERB	10	_____
VERB	11	_____
ADJECTIVE	12	_____
NOUN ASSOCIATED WITH THE GUY (PLURAL)	13	_____
NOUN ASSOCIATED WITH THE GUY (PLURAL)	14	_____
UNFLATTERING VERB	15	_____

1_____ was feeling, thinking, 2_____ about

3_____; 4_____, happy, miserable,

infinitely 5_____, absolutely 6_____. It

was all beyond belief! He was inexcusable, incomprehensible! But such

were his habits that he could do nothing without 7_____.

He had previously made her the happiest of 8_____, and

now he had 9_____—she knew not what to say, how to

10_____, or how to 11_____ it. She

would not have him be 12_____, and yet what could

excuse the use of such 13_____ and

14_____, if they meant but to 15_____?

SCANDALOUS!

THE GREATEST
(PAIN OF HIS) GENERATION

Fanny's uncle in *Mansfield Park* really likes Fanny, until she refuses to marry Henry and starts showing free will, independent thought, the ability to make decisions, and all those other things women are supposed to lose while they quilt and/or cook you dinner. In a contemporary setting, Uncle Old-Timer's opinions seem even more ridiculous. Fill in the blanks to hear him reminisce about the good old days when he would walk to school uphill both ways in the snow with no shoes. (Note: The no-shoes part is because his sister refused to put them on for him.)

ADVERB	1	_____
AN ACTIVITY OF A MODERN WOMAN (ENDING IN -ING)	2	_____
ANOTHER ACTIVITY OF A MODERN WOMAN (ENDING IN -ING)	3	_____
YOUR CITY	4	_____
YOUR OCCUPATION (PLURAL)	5	_____
SOMETHING GROSS (PLURAL)	6	_____
NEGATIVE ADJECTIVE	7	_____
ANOTHER ACTIVITY OF A MODERN WOMAN (ENDING IN -ING)	8	_____
SLANG FOR "OLD PEOPLE"	9	_____
AN ACTIVITY OLD PEOPLE LIKE	10	_____
SOMETHING OLD PEOPLE NEED	11	_____
SOMEONE WHO IS VERY PRIM AND PROPER (FICTIONAL, A CELEBRITY, OR A PERSONAL FRIEND)	12	_____

"I had thought you 1_____ free from

2_____, 3_____, and every tendency

to that independence of spirit which prevails so much in modern

4_____, even in 5_____, and

which in young women is offensive and disgusting beyond

6_____. But you have now shewn me that you can be

willful and 7_____; that you can and will

8_____ for yourself, without any consideration or

deference for 9_____ who have surely some right to

10_____—without even asking for their

11_____. You have shewn yourself very, very different

from 12_____."

MARY, MARY,
QUITE CONTRARY

Edmund's summation of Mary at the end of *Mansfield Park* boils down to this: She's not naturally cruel, she's just cruel because it's what people do. In other words, Mary's one of the mean girls. She's the Rachel McAdams to your Lindsay Lohan, and there's no Tina Fey to mediate the argument. Fine, then let's blow this out to its hair-pulling, name-calling, backstabbing, lipstick-wearing after-school special of a conclusion: Fill in the blanks to get all the high school drama.

A MEAN THING TO CALL A GIRL	1	_____
ADJECTIVE FORM OF THE WORD FROM #1	2	_____
SOMETHING A BAD GIRL WOULD DO	3	_____
SOMETHING THAT MIGHT STOP THE ACT FROM #3	4	_____
SLANG FOR A "FRIEND"	5	_____
A MEAN GIRL FROM YOUR HIGH SCHOOL	6	_____
A FEMALE VILLAIN FROM A HIGH SCHOOL MOVIE	7	_____
A FAMOUSLY HAUGHTY DESIGNER	8	_____
SLANG FOR "NERD"	9	_____
AN ITEM HIGH SCHOOL GIRLS WOULD BE JEALOUS OF	10	_____
A KNOCKOFF DESIGNER FOR TARGET OR WALMART	11	_____
VERB (PAST TENSE)	12	_____

1_____, do you call it? We differ there. No, hers is

not a 2_____ nature. I do not consider her as meaning

to 3_____. The evil lies yet deeper: in her total

ignorance, unsuspiciousness of there being 4_____;

in a perversion of mind which made it natural to her to treat

5_____as she did. She was speaking only as she had

been used to hear 6_____ speak, as she imagined

7_____ would speak. Hers are not faults of

8_____. She would not voluntarily give unnecessary

pain to 9_____, and though I may deceive myself,

I cannot but think that for me, for my 10_____,

she would—Hers are faults of 11_____, Fanny; of

blunted delicacy and a corrupted, 12_____ mind.

MANSFIELD-GATE

Love can make a guy do some crazy things. Like, you know, sneaking off to see his "soul mate" when he's supposed to be, oh, let's say, governing a state. With the help of your political reporting, Fanny's married cousin Maria, who runs off with the caddish Henry Crawford, can become embroiled in a juicy political scandal worthy of both CNN and the *National Enquirer*.

VERB MEANING "SEE" (PAST TENSE)	1	_____
ADVERB SUGGESTING SHOCK OR SURPRISE	2	_____
A CABLE NEWS NETWORK	3	_____
A MARRIED MALE POLITICIAN	4	_____
THE WIFE OF THE POLITICIAN FROM #4	5	_____
A POLITICAL GROUP (EXAMPLE: THE NRA, THE NATIONAL ORGANIZATION FOR WOMEN, ETC.)	6	_____
VERB MEANING "TRY" (PAST TENSE)	7	_____
ADJECTIVE	8	_____
A JOB TITLE	9	_____
AN INDUSTRY ASSOCIATED WITH THE JOB FROM #9	10	_____
AN ASSET A GOLD DIGGER LOOKS FOR (EXAMPLE: WEALTH, CONNECTIONS, ETC.)	11	_____
A POLITICIAN ASSOCIATED WITH THE POLITICIAN FROM #4	12	_____
THE POLITICIAN FROM #4	13	_____
A WELL-KNOWN NEWS ANCHOR OR TV PERSONALITY	14	_____

Fanny **1**_____ **2**_____ that "it was with

infinite concern **3**_____ had to announce to the world a

matrimonial fracas in the family of **4**_____ of Wimpole

Street; the beautiful **5**_____, whose name had not long

been enrolled in **6**_____, and who had **7**_____

to become so **8**_____ a **9**_____ in the

10_____ world, having quitted her husband's

11_____ in company with the well-known and captivating

12_____, the intimate friend and associate of

13_____, and it was not known even to **14**_____

whither they were gone."

ONE TIME I
SAW ALICIA SILVERSTONE IN A BURGER KING

L ook, I'm going to level with you right now. It's been a while since I read *Emma*, OK? Don't get all upset or anything. I mean, I'm not totally clueless. After all, I did see, well, *Clueless*. And that's the same story, right? Right. So let's all just do your author a favor here and put the story in a context I can understand, 'kay? Fill in the blanks to give *Emma* the Beverly Hills treatment.

VALLEY GIRL SLANG FOR "PRETTY"	1	_____
VALLEY GIRL SLANG FOR "SMART"	2	_____
VALLEY GIRL SLANG FOR "RICH"	3	_____
TYPE OF HOUSE OR DWELLING	4	_____
SMALL DOG BREED	5	_____
THE DISGUSTINGLY RICH NEIGHBORHOOD IN YOUR TOWN	6	_____
FANCY FOOD	7	_____
SOMETHING A DUMB BLONDE MIGHT LIKE	8	_____
ARTICLES OF CLOTHING (PLURAL)	9	_____
VERB (PAST TENSE)	10	_____

Emma Woodhouse, 1_____, 2_____,

and 3_____, with a comfortable 4_____

and happy 5_____, seemed to unite some of the best

blessings of 6_____; and had lived nearly twenty-one

years in the world with very little to distress or vex her. . . .

The real evils, indeed, of Emma's situation were the power of having

rather too much 7_____, and a disposition to think a

little too well of 8_____; these were the disadvantages

which threatened alloy to her many 9_____. The danger,

however, was at the present so 10_____,

that they did not by any means rank as misfortunes with her.

AUSTEN-TATIOUS!

CELEBS
WITH BENEFITS

Every single girl will recognize the predictable skin-crawling refrain she hears from her friends as soon as she goes on a second date with any guy who passes the not-drooling-on-his-shirt test: "When-ah-ya gonna get maaaa-riiied?" And yet it's totally OK for Brad and Angelina to have six kids together without putting a ring on it. What's up with that? Jane Austen's Emma was all over that double standard and knew which one she preferred.

ADJECTIVE IMPLYING NEGATIVE JUDGMENT (EXAMPLE: "DEPLORABLE")	1	_____
SYNONYM FOR "SMALL"	2	_____
SYNONYM FOR "UGLY"	3	_____
A TERM FOR PEOPLE WHO GOSSIP ABOUT OTHERS (PLURAL NOUN)	4	_____
A TABLOID TERM FOR A FAMOUS PERSON (EXAMPLE: STAR, A-LISTER, ETC.)	5	_____
GUSHING ADJECTIVE YOU'D SEE IN A TABLOID (EXAMPLE: "FABULOUS")	6	_____
ADJECTIVE TO DESCRIBE A MOM	7	_____
SYNONYM FOR "EQUALITY"	8	_____
VERB MEANING "SHRINK"	9	_____
VERB	10	_____
ADVERB	11	_____
ADJECTIVE	12	_____
ADJECTIVE	13	_____
ADJECTIVE	14	_____

"Never mind, Harriet, I shall not be a poor old maid; and it is poverty only which makes celibacy 1_____ to a generous public! A single woman, with a very 2_____ income, must be a ridiculous, 3_____ old maid! the proper sport of 4_____; but a single 5_____, of good fortune, is always respectable, and may be as 6_____ and 7_____ as anybody else. And the distinction is not quite so much against the 8_____ and common sense of the world as appears at first; for a very narrow income has a tendency to 9_____ the mind, and 10_____ the temper. Those who can barely live, and who live 11_____ in a very small, and generally very inferior, society, may well be 12_____ and cross. This does not apply, however, to Miss Bates; she is only too 13_____ and too 14_____ to suit me; but, in general, she is very much to the taste of everybody, though single and though poor."

BECAUSE
NO ONE WANTS
TO FEDEX A PIANO

There's this scene in *Emma* where everybody and their mother gets all hot and bothered by the fact that someone has sent Jane Fairfax a piano. Big whoop. I've had secret admirers send me oversized musical instruments as a sign of their love. Who hasn't? If you want to get a gal's attention, you have to go big or go home. You have to send something audacious, something clever, something egregiously expensive, something . . . well, fill in the blanks to find out what I mean.

A RIDICULOUSLY EXTRAVAGANT GIFT	1	_____
A MORE MODEST GIFT	2	_____
A FAST-FOOD SIZE (EXAMPLE: EXTRA-LARGE, JUMBO, VENTI, ETC.)	3	_____
AN UNUSUAL COLOR	4	_____
THE GIFT FROM #1	5	_____
A POSITIVE STATE OF BEING	6	_____
THE GIFT FROM #1	7	_____
A LAME CITY	8	_____
A FUNNY NAME	9	_____
ANOTHER FUNNY NAME	10	_____
ANOTHER FUNNY NAME	11	_____
AN OCCUPATION	12	_____
THE NAME OF SOMEONE WHO HAS #12'S OCCUPATION	13	_____

Mrs. Cole was telling us that she had been calling on Miss Bates, and as soon as she entered the room had been struck by the sight of a

1_____—a very elegant-looking instrument—not a

2_____, but a 3_____-sized

4_____ 5_____; and the substance of

the story, the end of all the dialogue which ensued of surprise, and

6_____, and congratulations on her side, and explana-

tions on Miss Bates's, was, that this 7_____ had arrived

from 8_____ the day before, to the great astonishment

of both 9_____ and 10_____—entirely

unexpected; that at first, by Miss Bates's account, 11_____

herself was quite at a loss, quite bewildered to think who could possibly

have ordered it—but now, they were both perfectly satisfied that it could

be from only one 12_____;—of course it must be from

13_____.

TO LIVE
AND DIE ON SESAME STREET

When Harriet is mugged by a band of gypsy children, her horror is met by a singular thought from the reader: Man up, Harriet; children are very easy to beat in a fight. Not to belittle the toughness of gypsies and their Eastern European heartiness, but it's not hard to push a kid and run. In fact, the only people easier to beat in a fight than children are children's *entertainers*. Fill in the blanks to see what happens when Harriet is attacked by PBS's finest.

A NONTHREATENING CITY	**1**	_____
A NONTHREATENING THING IN A PARK (PLURAL)	**2**	_____
ADJECTIVE	**3**	_____
A GROUP OF PEOPLE WHO SCARE EASILY (PLURAL)	**4**	_____
CHARACTERS ON A CHILDREN'S TELEVISION SHOW (PLURAL)	**5**	_____
THE NAME OF ONE OF THESE CHARACTERS	**6**	_____
THE NAME OF SOMEONE WHO SCARES EASILY	**7**	_____
A PIECE OF PLAYGROUND EQUIPMENT	**8**	_____
ANOTHER PIECE OF PLAYGROUND EQUIPMENT	**9**	_____
THE CITY FROM #1	**10**	_____
THE TV CHARACTERS FROM #5	**11**	_____
THE NAME OF A CHARACTER FROM #5	**12**	_____
ANOTHER NAME OF A CHARACTER FROM #5	**13**	_____
SOMETHING PUPPETS WOULD LIKE	**14**	_____
SOMETHING ELSE PUPPETS WOULD LIKE	**15**	_____

About half a mile beyond 1_____ , making a sudden turn, and deeply shaded by 2_____ on each side, it became for a considerable stretch very 3_____ ; and when the 4_____ had advanced some way into it, they had suddenly perceived, at a small distance before them . . . a party of 5_____ . 6_____ on the watch came towards them to beg; and 7_____ , excessively frightened, gave a great scream, and calling on Harriet to follow her, ran up a steep 8_____, cleared a slight 9_____ at the top, and made the best of her way by a short cut back to 10_____ . But poor Harriet could not follow. . . .

Harriet was soon assailed by half a dozen 11_____ , headed by a stout 12_____ and a great 13_____ , all clamorous, and impertinent in look, though not absolutely in word. More and more frightened, she immediately promised them 14_____ , and taking out her purse, gave them a 15_____ , and begged them not to want more, or to use her ill. She was then able to walk, though but slowly, and was moving away—but her terror and her purse were too tempting, and she was followed, or rather surrounded, by the whole gang, demanding more.

HARRIET:
A FEW PAGES SHORT OF A JANE AUSTEN NOVEL

Within every friend group, there's a charity case, the one person who's a little bit . . . special. There's always a Lennie who keeps asking George to pet the rabbits, and there's always a Steve Carrell in *Anchorman* who insists that he "ate a big red candle" at inopportune times. Well, for Emma, Harriet is that person. Remember when she couldn't beat back a group of children? Ah, memories. Fill in the blanks to learn about that "special" someone, whether they're in your group of friends or not.

SOMEONE SMART (OR AT LEAST SOMEONE WHO THINKS THEY ARE)	1	_____
ADVERB	2	_____
ADVERB	3	_____
SLANG FOR "IDIOT"	4	_____
A STATUS SYMBOL	5	_____
ANOTHER STATUS SYMBOL	6	_____
ANOTHER STATUS SYMBOL	7	_____
A VERY SMALL CREATURE OR BUG	8	_____
COMMON PHRASE TO SHOW DIMNESS (EXAMPLE: "A FEW CRAYONS SHORT," "ONE APPLE SHORT OF A BARREL," ETC.)	9	_____
ANOTHER COMMON PHRASE TO SHOW DIMNESS	10	_____
ANOTHER COMMON PHRASE TO SHOW DIMNESS	11	_____
NEGATIVE ADJECTIVE	12	_____
NEGATIVE ADJECTIVE	13	_____
NOUN (PLURAL)	14	_____

"Not Harriet's equal!" exclaimed 1_____ 2_____ and 3_____; and with calmer asperity, added, a few moments afterwards, "No, he is not her equal indeed, for he is as much her superior in sense as in situation. Emma, your infatuation about that 4_____ blinds you. What are Harriet Smith's claims, either of 5_____, 6_____ or 7_____, to any connection higher than a[an]8_____? She is 9_____. She is 10_____. She is 11_____. She has been taught nothing useful, and is too 12_____ and too 13_____ to have acquired any thing herself. At her age she can have no 14_____, and with her little wit, is not very likely ever to have any that can avail her. She is pretty, and she is good tempered, and that is all."

NO, CONSTABLE, I HAVEN'T BEEN DRINKING

Drunk texting or e-mailing your crush is a bad idea. Drunk dialing them is an even worse one. That said, none of these hold a candle to drunk carriage-riding with your crush, and yet it seems that is exactly what Elton does in *Emma* (though he'll deny the drinking bit). Fill in the blanks to update this classically uncomfortable moment into a thoroughly modern and still completely awkward affair.

YOUR HARD-PARTYING FRIEND	1	_____
A POTENT LIQUOR	2	_____
SYNONYM FOR "GIBBERISH"	3	_____
A CURRENT EVENT	4	_____
ANOTHER CURRENT EVENT	5	_____
AN UNIMPRESSIVE LANDMARK IN YOUR AREA	6	_____
A FREEWAY IN YOUR AREA	7	_____
VERB (ENDING IN -ING)	8	_____
VERB (ENDING IN -ING)	9	_____
VERB (ENDING IN -ING)	10	_____
VERB	11	_____
ADJECTIVE	12	_____
ADJECTIVE	13	_____
ADJECTIVE	14	_____
A DISMISSIVE TERM (EXAMPLE: HOGWASH, CRAP, ETC.)	15	_____

But now, she would rather it had not happened. She believed he had been drinking too much of 1_____'s good 2_____, and felt sure that he would want to be talking 3_____.

To restrain him as much as might be, by her own manners, she was immediately preparing to speak with exquisite calmness and gravity of 4_____ and 5_____; but scarcely had she begun, scarcely had they passed the 6_____ and joined the 7_____, than she found her subject cut up—her hand seized—her attention demanded, and Mr. Elton actually making violent love to her: availing himself of the precious opportunity, declaring sentiments which must be already well known, 8_____—9_____—10_____—ready to 11_____ if she refused him; but flattering himself that his 12_____ attachment and 13_____ love and 14_____ passion could not fail of having some effect, and in short, very much resolved on being seriously accepted as soon as possible. It really was so. . . . She felt that half this 15_____ must be drunkenness, and therefore could hope that it might belong only to the passing hour.

YOU SHOULD
GET THAT CHECKED OUT

In chapter 24 of *Emma*, Frank Churchill and Emma have the vain conversation to end all vain conversations regarding the unsightliness of Jane Fairfax's complexion. She's really just a little bit pale, but the way Frank and Emma talk about her, you'd think she had elephantiasis. So let's try to justify the conversation by really going all-out on Jane's complexion. Fill in the blanks to read about a face that could send the Clearasil research department into bankruptcy.

NEGATIVE ADJECTIVE	1	_____
THE ADJECTIVE FROM #1	2	_____
THE ADJECTIVE FROM #1	3	_____
ANOTHER NEGATIVE ADJECTIVE	4	_____
ANOTHER NEGATIVE ADJECTIVE	5	_____
UNATTRACTIVE NOUN	6	_____
UNATTRACTIVE NOUN	7	_____
SYNONYM FOR "WEAK"	8	_____
SLANG FOR "SEXY"	9	_____
A COLOR	10	_____
AN ANIMAL	11	_____
A VEGETABLE (PLURAL)	12	_____
AN UNSAVORY OCCUPATION (PLURAL)	13	_____
SYNONYM FOR "LOTS" (EXAMPLE: OODLES, TONS, MASS AMOUNTS, ETC.)	14	_____
SOMETHING GROSS FOUND ON FACES	15	_____

"And how did you think Miss Fairfax looking?"

"**1**_____, very **2**_____—that is, if a young lady can ever be allowed to look **3**_____. But the expression is hardly admissible, Mrs. Weston, is it? Ladies can never look **4**_____. And, seriously, Miss Fairfax is naturally so **5**_____, as almost always to give the appearance of **6**_____.—A most deplorable **7**_____ of complexion."

Emma would not agree to this, and began a[n] **8**_____ defense of Miss Fairfax's complexion. "It was certainly never **9**_____, but she would not allow it to have a **10**_____ hue in general; and there was a **11**_____ and **12**_____ in her skin which gave peculiar elegance to the character of her face." He listened with all due deference; acknowledged that he had heard many **13**_____ say the same—but yet he must confess, that to him nothing could make amends for **14**_____ of **15**_____.

BOY,
YOU ARE LOOKING GOOD ON THAT PLAYGROUND...

The way Elinor speaks of Edward in *Sense and Sensibility*—calmly, coolly, without admitting that she actually likes him—has a certain finesse to it. That finesse can also be found in a fourth-grader who pulls the hair of the boy she likes before running around the schoolyard screaming about how he gave her cooties. Fill in the blanks to read about Elinor's playground passion for Edward.

A SCHOOLYARD GAME	1	_____
THE GAME FROM #1	2	_____
A TOY THAT BOYS LIKE (PLURAL)	3	_____
ANOTHER TOY THAT BOYS LIKE (PLURAL)	4	_____
A SUGAR-FILLED SNACK	5	_____
SYNONYM FOR "EXCITED"	6	_____
AN ARTICLE OF CHILDREN'S CLOTHING	7	_____
A BODY PART	8	_____
A SATURDAY-MORNING CARTOON	9	_____
ANOTHER SATURDAY MORNING CARTOON	10	_____
ADJECTIVE A KID WOULD USE	11	_____
A KIDS' BOARD GAME	12	_____
A GAME KIDS PLAY	13	_____
ADJECTIVE	14	_____
A BODY PART	15	_____
A BODY PART	16	_____
BODY PARTS (PLURAL)	17	_____
A TYPE OF CANDY	18	_____

"Of his sense and his 1_____," continued Elinor, "no one can, I think, be in doubt, who has seen him often enough to engage him in unreserved 2_____. The excellence of his 3_____ and his 4_____ can be concealed only by that 5_____ which too often keeps him 6_____. You know enough of him to do justice to his 7_____. . . . I have seen a great deal of him, have studied his 8_____, and heard his opinion on subjects of 9_____ and 10_____; and, upon the whole, I venture to pronounce that his mind is 11_____, his enjoyment of 12_____ exceedingly great, his imagination lively, his 13_____ just and correct, and his taste 14_____ and pure. His abilities in every respect improve as much upon acquaintance as his manners and person. At first sight, his 15_____ is certainly not striking; and his 16_____ can hardly be called handsome, till the expression of his 17_____, which are uncommonly good, and the general sweetness of his 18_____, is perceived. At present, I know him so well, that I think him really handsome; or, at least, almost so. What say you, Marianne?"

CENTS
AND SALABILITY

It's one thing when two women bicker over a guy. It's quite another thing to see two women bicker over who should take the last blender on the discount rack at Sears. There is feigned politeness, the insistence that you'll ask the clerk if there are more in the back, and the secret hope that the other person will lose interest so that you can make a mad dash for the checkout line. Fill in the blanks to see what happens when Elinor and Marianne butt heads during a shopping spree.

ADJECTIVE TO DESCRIBE AN APPLIANCE	1	_____
SOMETHING YOU WOULD BUY AT SEARS	2	_____
A PART OF THE THING FROM #2	3	_____
ANOTHER PART OF THE THING FROM #2	4	_____
SYNONYM FOR "CONNED"	5	_____
A CAMPY BRAND NAME FOR THE THING FROM #2 (EXAMPLE: BLEND-O 3000)	6	_____
THE NAME FROM #6	7	_____
ADJECTIVE	8	_____
ADJECTIVE	9	_____
ADJECTIVE	10	_____
THE NAME FROM #6	11	_____
THE NAME FROM #6	12	_____
A TOOTHLESS INSULT	13	_____
THE INSULT FROM #13	14	_____
A DEPARTMENT STORE SECTION	15	_____

"I shall very soon think [it] 1_____, Elinor, if I do not now. When you tell me to love [it] as a 2_____, I shall no more see imperfection in [its] 3_____ than I now do in [its] 4_____."

Elinor started at this declaration, and was sorry for the warmth she had been 5_____ into in speaking of 6_____. She felt that 7_____ stood very 8_____ in her opinion. She believed the regard to be 9_____; but she required greater certainty of it to make Marianne's conviction of their attachment 10_____ to her. . . .

"I do not attempt to deny," said she, "that I think very highly of 11_____—that I greatly esteem, that I like 12_____."

Marianne here burst forth with indignation—

"Esteem [it]! Like [it]! 13_____ Elinor! Oh! worse than 14_____! Ashamed of being otherwise. Use those words again, and I will leave the 15_____ this moment."

JANE AUSTEN:
HARLEQUIN FREELANCER

On the whole, Jane Austen's work is very concerned with appearance and respectability and all things prim and proper. But every so often, you just want those simmering passages to boil over into . . . *trashy*. Oh sure, she tries to hide it behind English country homes and respectable families of means, but take this passage from *Sense and Sensibility* in which she describes Wickham's "manly beauty." It's clear that Miss Austen has a bodice ripper just waiting in the wings, so let's fill in the blanks to sultry it up!

SEXY ADJECTIVE	1	_____
A PLACE OF LOOSE MORALS	2	_____
SEXY ADJECTIVE	3	_____
A BODY PART	4	_____
A BODY PART	5	_____
SULTRY VERB (ENDING IN -ING)	6	_____
VERB SIMILAR TO LOOKING, STARING, ETC. (ENDING IN -ING)	7	_____
A SEXY LOCATION	8	_____
AN ATTRACTIVE PART OF A MAN	9	_____
ANOTHER ATTRACTIVE PART OF A MAN	10	_____
A BAD ROMANCE MOVIE	11	_____
THE PLACE FROM #8	12	_____
SOMETHING YOU DO ON A FIRST DATE	13	_____
AN ITEM A MAN WOULD OWN	14	_____
THE NAME OF YOUR FAVORITE MALE TEACHER	15	_____
YOUR NEIGHBORHOOD	16	_____
AN ITEM OF MEN'S CLOTHING	17	_____

The gentleman offered his services; and perceiving that her modesty declined what her situation rendered 1_____, took her up in his arms, without farther delay, and carried her down [to] the 2_____. . . .

His manly beauty and more than 3_____ 4_____ were instantly the theme of general admiration; and the laugh which his gallantry raised against Marianne received particular spirit from his exterior attractions. Marianne herself had seen less of his 5_____ than the rest, for the confusion which crimsoned over her face, on his 6_____ her up, had robbed her of the power of 7_____ him after their entering the 8_____. But she had seen enough of him to join in all the admiration of the others, and with an energy which always adorned her praise. His 9_____ and 10_____ were equal to what her fancy had ever drawn for the hero of 11_____; and in his carrying her into the 12_____ with so little previous 13_____ there was a rapidity of thought which particularly recommended the action to her. Every 14_____ belonging to him was interesting. His name was 15_____, his residence was in 16_____, and she soon found out that of all manly dresses a 17_____ was the most becoming.

DEAR LOVE, PLEASE TAKE IT DOWN A NOTCH. SINCERELY, *Sensibility*

L ove has always left us in a state of excitement, with hearts and other body parts aflutter. But in the modern age, with racier movies, goofier reality shows, and epically long Facebook comment strings when someone's status changes to "In a relationship," we are getting dramarama 24/7 when it comes to the L word. So, to update this *Sense and Sensibility* passage for today's reader, remember to spell "love" L-Omg-V-E.

A FEMALE NAME	1	_____
ANOTHER FEMALE NAME	2	_____
SLANG FOR "MARRIED"	3	_____
A HUNKY MALE NAME	4	_____
SLANG FOR "ANXIETY" (EXAMPLE: JITTERS)	5	_____
ADVERB	6	_____
SLANG FOR "RELAXED"	7	_____
SYNONYM FOR "DOUBT"	8	_____
MORE SLANG FOR "ANXIETY"	9	_____
ADVERB	10	_____
SLANG FOR "INTERESTED IN" (EXAMPLE: DIGGING, DOWN WITH, ETC.)	11	_____
SYNONYM FOR "AFFECTION" OR "LOVE"	12	_____
SLANG FOR "PASSIONATE" OR "SEXY"	13	_____
SLANG FOR "CONSTANT" (EXAMPLE: AROUND THE CLOCK)	14	_____
SLANG FOR "EXCITED"	15	_____
SLANG FOR "HAPPINESS"	16	_____
SLANG FOR "RELAXATION"	17	_____
MORE SLANG FOR "RELAXATION"	18	_____

But 1_____—how are *her* feelings to be described? From the moment of learning that 2_____ was 3_____ to another, that 4_____ was free, to the moment of his justifying the 5_____ which had so 6_____ followed, she was every thing by turns but 7_____. But when the second moment had passed, when she found every 8_____, every 9_____ removed, compared her situation with what so lately it had been,—saw him 10_____ released from his former engagement,—saw him instantly 11_____ the release, to address herself and declare a[n] 12_____ as 13_____, as 14_____ as she had ever supposed it to be,—she was 15_____, she was overcome by her own 16_____; and happily disposed as is the human mind to be easily familiarized with any change for the better, it required several hours to give 17_____ to her spirits, or any degree of 18_____ to her heart.

SENSE AND SENSIBILITY:
MONEY NEVER SLEEPS

Sisters rarely see eye to eye; Elinor and Marianne are no exception, especially when it comes to money. Elinor seems to know what a comfortable life can be, while Marianne expects nothing less than the best. To put it another way, Elinor knows her budget at Target, while Marianne assumes European vacations and on-call nutritionists are all part of middle-class life. Fill in the blanks for a sisterly dispute over household economics.

A RICH PERSON	1	_____
SLANG FOR "MONEY"	2	_____
SYNONYM/SLANG FOR "FAME"	3	_____
THE WORD FROM #3	4	_____
A FAMOUSLY UNSCRUPULOUS RICH PERSON	5	_____
SLANG FOR "MONEY"	6	_____
THE PERSON FROM #5	7	_____
THE PERSON FROM #1	8	_____
A FORM OF PASSIVE INCOME (EXAMPLE: TRUST FUND, STOCK PORTFOLIO, ETC.)	9	_____
THE PERSON FROM #5	10	_____
THE FORM OF INCOME FROM #9	11	_____
AN EGREGIOUSLY EXPENSIVE AND SILLY LUXURY	12	_____
THE FORM OF INCOME FROM #9	13	_____
A HUGE AMOUNT OF MONEY	14	_____
THE PERSON FROM #5	15	_____
THE AMOUNT OF MONEY FROM #14	16	_____
A SLIGHTLY SMALLER AMOUNT OF MONEY THAN IN #14	17	_____
A TACKY LUXURY ITEM	18	_____
THE AMOUNT OF MONEY FROM #14	19	_____
THE PERSON FROM #1	20	_____
SOME SORT OF HIRED HELP (PLURAL)	21	_____
AN EXTRAVAGANT LUXURY	22	_____
UNNECESSARY HIRED HELP (PLURAL)	23	_____

"Strange if it would!" cried 1_____. "What have

2_____ or 3_____ to do with happiness?"

"4_____ has but little," said 5_____,

"but 6_____ has much to do with it."

"7_____, for shame!" said 8_____;

"money can only give happiness where there is nothing else to give it.

Beyond a 9_____, it can afford no real satisfaction, as far

as mere self is concerned."

"Perhaps," said 10_____, smiling, "we may come to

the same point. _Your_ 11_____ and _my_

12_____ are very much alike, I dare say. . . Come, what

is your 13_____?"

"About 14_____ a year; not more than _that_."

15_____ laughed. "16_____ a year!

17_____ is my 18_____! I guessed how

it would end."

"And yet 19_____ a year is a very moderate income,"

said 20_____. "A family cannot well be maintained on a

smaller. I am sure I am not extravagant in my demands. A proper

establishment of 21_____, a[n]

22_____, perhaps two, and 23_____,

cannot be supported on less."

SENSE AND SENSIBILITY:
HOTLANTA EDITON

When Elinor and Marianne meet the Steeles, they are overtaken by the stench of feigned politeness. The Steeles employ a kind of sugary manner that is so sweet it can only be intended to give you diabetes. It brings to mind the nature of a Southern belle who's incredibly nice to you in person, but would say whatever she needed to about you to get box seats to the Daughters of the Confederacy Sunday picnic and fashion show. Fill in the blanks to get way too much of that famed Southern hospitality.

A SOUTHERN CITY	1	_____
A NUMBER	2	_____
ADJECTIVE	3	_____
A PLANTATION ACCESSORY	4	_____
A SMALLER NUMBER THAN IN #2	5	_____
A BODY PART	6	_____
NOUN (PLURAL)	7	_____
SOMETHING FOUND ON A PLANTATION (PLURAL)	8	_____
A MONIKER FOR SOMEONE FROM A SOUTHERN STATE (EXAMPLE: GEORGIAN, VIRGINIAN, ETC.)	9	_____
A LANDMARK IN #9'S STATE	10	_____
A FEMALE COUNTRY STAR	11	_____
A TOY (PLURAL)	12	_____
MEMBERS OF THE SERVICE INDUSTRY (PLURAL)	13	_____
A NICKNAME FOR #11	14	_____
AN ITEM OF FARM CLOTHING	15	_____

When their promised visit to 1_____, and consequent introduction to these young ladies, took place, they found in the appearance of the eldest, who was nearly 2_____, with a very 3_____ and not a sensible 4_____, nothing to admire; but in the other, who was not more than 5_____, they acknowledged considerable beauty: her features were pretty, and she had a sharp quick 6_____, and a smartness of air, which though it did not give actual 7_____ or 8_____, gave distinction to her person. Their manners were particularly 9_____, and Elinor soon allowed them credit for 10_____, when she saw with what constant and judicious attention they were making themselves agreeable to 11_____. With her children they were in continual raptures, extolling their 12_____, courting their notice, and humoring all their 13_____; and such of their time as could be spared from the importunate demands which this politeness made on it, was spent in admiration of whatever 14_____ was doing, if she happened to be doing anything, or in taking patterns of some elegant new 15_____, in which her appearance the day before had thrown them into unceasing delight."

OVER THE HILL
AND OVER THE TOP

When Marianne and Elinor meet Mrs. Jennings, they are surprised that she is a very jovial and foulmouthed member of the geriatric community. It's as if Joan Rivers and Betty White pulled out a Ouija board to tell dirty jokes to George Burns. Fill in the blanks to meet one foul-minded blue-hair.

AN OLD CELEBRITY	1	_____
ADJECTIVE	2	_____
ADJECTIVE	3	_____
ADJECTIVE	4	_____
A STATE OF BEING	5	_____
A SWEAR WORD OR EXCLAMATION (PLURAL)	6	_____
ANOTHER SWEAR WORD OR EXCLAMATION (PLURAL)	7	_____
A DAYTIME TALK SHOW	8	_____
A SOAP OPERA	9	_____
A CITY	10	_____
A LEWD ACTION	11	_____
SYNONYM FOR "JOKES"	12	_____
SYNONYM FOR "ANTICS"	13	_____

Mrs. Jennings, **1**_____'s mother, was a **2**_____,

3_____, **4**_____, elderly woman, who

talked a great deal, seemed very **5**_____, and rather

vulgar. She was full of **6**_____ and

7_____, and before dinner was over had said many witty

things on the subject of **8**_____ and

9_____; hoped they had not left their hearts behind

them in **10**_____, and pretended to see them

11_____ whether they did or not. Marianne was vexed at

it for her sister's sake, and turned her eyes towards Elinor to see how she

bore these **12**_____, with an earnestness which gave

Elinor far more pain than could arise from such common-place

13_____ as Mrs. Jennings's.

NORTHANGER ABBEY
IS FOR LOVERS
(OF COMPLETE BOREDOM)

I n *Northanger Abbey*, Catherine is beside herself in excitement over her visit to the estate named in the title. But Northanger Abbey is in Bath, England. Plain old Bath. Sorry, Bath, but at the time of this writing, Bath's city website was promoting a parking lot with 876 spaces as a noteworthy attraction. It's as if Catherine were excited to visit Cleveland, or it's like when your boyfriend took you to "the most awesome take-out place" in his hometown, and the woman behind the counter didn't wear a hairnet and took your order between drags of her cigarette. Let's call a spade a spade. Fill in the blanks to see someone get *waaaaay* too excited about a lame place.

A VERY BORING LOCATION	1	_____
A PERSON YOU KNOW WHO WOULD LIKE THIS LOCATION	2	_____
POSSESSIVE PRONOUN FOR THE PERSON FROM #2	3	_____
A BODY PART	4	_____
ADJECTIVE	5	_____
A STATE OF BEING (EXAMPLE: HAPPINESS, SADNESS, ANGER, ETC.)	6	_____
THE PRONOUN FROM #3	7	_____
SOMETHING THE PERSON FROM #2 MAKES AT THEIR PLACE OF WORK	8	_____
ADJECTIVE	9	_____
ADJECTIVE	10	_____
THE PRONOUN FROM #3	11	_____
A PERSON CLOSE TO THE PERSON FROM #2	12	_____
ANOTHER PERSON CLOSE TO THE PERSON FROM #2	13	_____
WHERE THE PEOPLE FROM #12 AND #13 LIVE	14	_____
THE PRONOUN FROM #3	15	_____

1_____! These were thrilling words, and wound up
2_____'s feelings to the highest point of ecstasy.
3_____grateful and gratified 4_____ could
hardly restrain its expressions within the language of
5_____ 6_____. To receive so flattering an
invitation! To have 7_____ 8_____ so
warmly solicited! Everything 9_____ and
10_____, every present enjoyment, and every future hope
was contained in it; and 11_____ acceptance, with only the
saving clause of 12_____ and 13_____'s
approbation, was eagerly given. "I will write 14_____
directly," said 15_____, "and if they do not object, as I dare
say they will not—"

'MEMBER, GUV, WE'RE ENGLISH

I n *Northanger Abbey*, Catherine is reminded to tone it down on some of her racier theories regarding the death of Mrs. Tilney. She is told that she should hold herself back: "Remember, we are English." How easy to forget that while England is certainly tea and crumpets, it is also ales and meat pies. England is football hooligans and cockney pickpockets and blokes who knock your teeth out because you look at them funny. Fill in the blanks to remember what it means to be English.

A CELEBRITY WITH A COCKNEY ACCENT	1	_____
BRITISH SLANG FOR "BAD"	2	_____
A PLACE WHERE HOOLIGANS HANG OUT	3	_____
ANOTHER PLACE WHERE HOOLIGANS HANG OUT	4	_____
VERB (PAST TENSE)	5	_____
SYNONYM FOR "TROUBLEMAKERS"	6	_____
SOMETHING A BLOKE OWNS	7	_____
SOMETHING A GEEZER HAS	8	_____
SYNONYM FOR "MATES"	9	_____
A BRITISH SOCCER TEAM	10	_____
SOMETHING FOR NUTTERS (PLURAL)	11	_____
A NEIGHBORHOOD IN LONDON	12	_____
ADJECTIVE	13	_____
AN OCCUPATION THAT SEEMS BRITISH (PLURAL)	14	_____
NOUN (PLURAL)	15	_____
NOUN (PLURAL)	16	_____

"If I understand you rightly, you had formed a surmise of such horror as I have hardly words to—Dear 1_____, consider the 2_____ nature of the suspicions you have entertained. What have you been judging from? Remember the 3_____ and the 4_____ in which we 5_____. Remember that we are English, that we are 6_____. Consult your 7_____, your own 8_____, your own 9_____. Does our 10_____ prepare us for such atrocities? Do our 11_____ connive at them? Could they be perpetrated without being known, in 12_____ like this, where 13_____ intercourse is on such a footing; where every man is surrounded by a neighborhood of 14_____; and where 15_____ and 16_____ lay everything open?"

NORTHANGER ABBEY
AND ZOMBIES
AND SEA MONSTERS
AND ALL THAT STUFF

R emember those books *Pride and Prejudice and Zombies*, then *Sense and Sensibility and Sea Monsters*? Yeah, that was totally my idea until that dude stole it and started selling the books in Urban Outfitters stores everywhere. *My* version was way better. Ask yourself what scares the bejeezus out of you? Now ask yourself if you'd like to see it in *Northanger Abbey*. You bet your delicious brains you would! Fill in the blanks to make it happen.

CREEPY ADJECTIVE	1	_____
A SUPERNATURAL CREATURE	2	_____
ANOTHER SUPERNATURAL CREATURE	3	_____
SUPERNATURAL CREATURES (PLURAL)	4	_____
A CREEPY LOCATION	5	_____
SYNONYM FOR "REST"	6	_____
SYNONYM FOR "MYSTERIOUSLY"	7	_____
ADJECTIVE	8	_____
ADJECTIVE	9	_____
A STATE OF BEING (EXAMPLE: HAPPINESS, ANGER, CONFUSION, ETC.)	10	_____
TYPE OF MONSTER (PLURAL)	11	_____

She paused a moment in 1_____ wonder. The

2_____ roared down the chimney, the 3_____

beat in torrents against the windows, and 4_____ seemed

to speak the awfulness of her situation. To retire to 5_____,

however, unsatisfied on such a point, would be vain, since

6_____ must be impossible with the consciousness of a

cabinet so 7_____ closed in her immediate vicinity. Again,

therefore, she applied herself to the key, and after moving it in every

8_____ way for some instants, with the

9_____ 10_____ of 11_____,

the door suddenly yielded to her hand.

SIMPLY SHOCKING!

NORTHANGER ABBEY:
NEW YORK TIMES
BESTSELLER

The *Mysteries of Udolpho* was written in 1794 by Ann Radcliffe. It was her fourth book, her most popular novel, and the mere mention of it bores me to tears. So to hear it mentioned in *Northanger Abbey* does not tingle my literary toes. To be honest, the last book I "read" was *Eat, Pray, Love*, which I paid twelve bucks to have Julia Roberts act out for me. So do me a favor and update this *Northanger Abbey* passage with books that I might actually want to ~~read~~ see as a movie. Thanks!

ANSWER #3 FIRST, THEN NAME A CHARACTER FROM #3	1	_____
ANOTHER CHARACTER FROM # 3	2	_____
A HUGE BESTSELLER OF A BOOK	3	_____
ADJECTIVE	4	_____
A PUBLICATION OR TYPE OF BOOK THAT DUDES READ	5	_____
AN OCCUPATION	6	_____
A PHRASE OR SLANG FOR "UNINTELLIGENT PERSON"	7	_____
A MASSIVELY BESTSELLING AUTHOR	8	_____
A STATE OF BEING (EXAMPLE: HAPPINESS, SADNESS, ANGER, ETC.)	9	_____
A MASSIVELY BESTSELLING BOOK	10	_____
A NUMBER	11	_____
A BODY PART	12	_____
A HOUSEHOLD CHORE (VERB + NOUN PHRASE)	13	_____
A NONGEOGRAPHICAL LOCATION	14	_____

"Oh no, I only mean what I have read about. It always puts me in mind of the country that **1**_____ and **2**_____ traveled through, in **3**_____. But you never read novels, I dare say?"

"Why not?"

"Because they are not **4**_____ enough for you—gentlemen read **5**_____."

"The person, be it gentleman or **6**_____, who has not pleasure in a good novel, must be **7**_____. I have read all **8**_____'s works, and most of them with great **9**_____. **10**_____, when I had once begun it, I could not lay down again; I remember finishing it in **11**_____ days—my **12**_____ standing on end the whole time."

"Yes," added Miss Tilney, "and I remember that you undertook to read it aloud to me, and that when I was called away for only five minutes to **13**_____, instead of waiting for me, you took the volume into the **14**_____, and I was obliged to stay till you had finished it."

UGH...
FIREFIGHTERS ARE SO LAST YEAR

I n this day and age, there are too many self-proclaimed nerds. People are getting excited about meeting people in professions that, frankly, are *waaaaay* too nerdy. Right now, someone's getting excited about their date with the librarian, someone's stoked to go drinking with the Flash game designer, and there's a party desperately awaiting the arrival of the IT guy for Craigslist. Well, they were doing it centuries ago too. Fill in the blanks to hear *Northanger Abbey*'s Eleanor geek out over some dweeb or another.

A TOTALLY NERDY PROFESSION (PLURAL)	1	_____
A FRIEND WHO'S "TOO COOL FOR SCHOOL"	2	_____
SOMETHING USED IN THE PROFESSION FROM #1	3	_____
SOMETHING CENTRAL TO THIS PROFESSION	4	_____
SOMETHING ELSE USED IN THIS PROFESSION	5	_____
SOMETHING ELSE USED IN THIS PROFESSION	6	_____
AN ACTIVITY OF THIS PROFESSION (EXAMPLE: MOON WALKING, FIREFIGHTING, ETC.)	7	_____
SOMETHING USED IN THIS PROFESSION (PLURAL)	8	_____
A DOCUMENT THIS PROFESSION USES	9	_____
A FAMOUS MEMBER OF THIS PROFESSION	10	_____
ANOTHER FAMOUS MEMBER OF THIS PROFESSION	11	_____
ANOTHER FAMOUS MEMBER OF THIS PROFESSION	12	_____
SOMEONE IN THIS PROFESSION	13	_____
SOMEONE ELSE IN THIS PROFESSION	14	_____

"1_____, you think," said 2_____, "are not happy in their flights of fancy. They display 3_____ without raising interest. I am fond of [the] 4_____, and am very well contented to take the 5_____ with the 6_____. In the principal 7_____ they have sources of intelligence in former histories and records, which may be as much depended on, I conclude, as anything that does not actually pass under one's own observation; and as for the little 8_____ you speak of, they are embellishments, and I like them as such. If a 9_____ be well drawn up, I read it with pleasure, by whomsoever it may be made—and probably with much greater, if the production of 10_____ or 11_____, than if the genuine words of 12_____, 13_____, or 14_____."

SIGMA CHI—
NORTHANGER ABBEY CHAPTER

You know those kind of fellows who boast about their keg-stand times and beer-pong skills and how they can burp the alphabet? You can generally find them covered in a thick layer of Axe body spray masking a lingering odor of stale PBR. Unfortunately, our fair heroine of *Northanger Abbey*, Catherine, is stuck in a carriage with just such a bro-man: John Thorpe.

A MAJOR PARTY SCHOOL OR FRATERNITY **1** _____

THE SCHOOL/FRAT FROM #1 **2** _____

A SLANG TERM FOR "MAN"
(EXAMPLE: DUDE, GUY, ETC.) **3** _____

A LARGE NUMBER **4** _____

ADJECTIVE A "DUDE" WOULD USE
(EXAMPLE: RADICAL, AWESOME, GNARLY, ETC.) **5** _____

SYNONYM FOR "PARTY" (NOUN) **6** _____

A NUMBER EVEN LARGER THAN THE ONE IN #4 **7** _____

A PHRASE TO DESCRIBE AN EPIC PARTY **8** _____

VERB OR VERB PHRASE MEANING "DRINK"
(EXAMPLE: CHUG, KNOCK BACK, ETC.) **9** _____

A CONSERVATIVE SCHOOL **10** _____

"1_____! There is no drinking at 2_____ now, I assure you. Nobody drinks there. You would hardly meet with a 3_____ who goes beyond his 4_____ pints at the utmost. Now, for instance, it was reckoned a[n] 5_____ thing at the last 6_____ in my rooms, that upon an average we cleared about 7_____ pints a head. It was looked upon as 8_____. *Mine* is famous good stuff, to be sure. You would not often 9_____ anything like it in 10_____."

OUTRAGEOUS!

:O OMG, MR. ELLIOT IS SO HOTTT!!! :O

When Anne develops a crush on Mr. Elliot in *Persuasion*, it's sweet . . . too sweet . . . sickeningly sweet. It's like peering into the diary of a sixth-grade girl. "He is so dreamy!!! :P!!!!!!!" It doesn't take much work to reimagine Anne as a puberty-stricken ball of hormones and pop songs. Fill in the blanks to make these changes a pink and sparkly reality.

POSITIVE ADJECTIVE	1	_____
SOMETHING IN A PRETEEN GIRL'S ROOM	2	_____
A POSITIVE STATE OF BEING (EXAMPLE: HAPPINESS, GLEE, ETC.)	3	_____
ANOTHER THING IN A PRETEEN GIRL'S ROOM	4	_____
ANOTHER POSITIVE STATE OF BEING	5	_____
ANOTHER THING IN A PRETEEN GIRL'S ROOM	6	_____
ANOTHER POSITIVE STATE OF BEING	7	_____
ANOTHER THING IN A PRETEEN GIRL'S ROOM	8	_____
A MUSICAL ACT PRETEENS LOVE	9	_____
A SONG BY THE MUSICAL ACT IN #9	10	_____
ANOTHER SONG BY THE MUSICAL ACT IN #9	11	_____
THE NAME OF A STUFFED ANIMAL	12	_____
AN ITEM FOUND AT A SLUMBER PARTY	13	_____

Anne's mind was in a most 1_____ state for the entertainment of the evening: it was just occupation enough: she had feelings for the 2_____, 3_____ for the 4_____, 5_____ for the 6_____, and 7_____ for the 8_____; and had never liked 9_____ better, at least during 10_____. Towards the close of it, in the interval succeeding 11_____, she explained the words of the song to 12_____. They had a 13_____ between them.

SCANDALOUS!

WHAT HAPPENS
IN ~~VEGAS~~ BATH
STAYS IN ~~VEGAS~~ BATH

The tone in this passage from *Persuasion* makes it sound like every young marriage is the by-product of a night of hard partying and harder drinking. It's like every wedding is unplanned and haphazard and officiated by an Elvis impersonator off the Strip. Well, no offense, Jane, but Bath could use a little spicing up. So if a spur-of-the-moment, Las Vegas–style wedding is what we need to get Bath kicking, then bring on the booze, the gambling, and the dancers. Especially the dancers.

AN OCCUPATION (PLURAL)	1	_____
A TIME WAY PAST YOUR BEDTIME	2	_____
ADJECTIVE	3	_____
ADJECTIVE	4	_____
SUGGESTIVE ADJECTIVE	5	_____
A BODY PART	6	_____
SLANG FOR "ESSENCE" (EXAMPLE: MOJO, VOODOO, ETC.)	7	_____
THE NAME OF A FAMOUS GUY IN LAS VEGAS	8	_____
THE NAME OF A FAMOUS GIRL IN LAS VEGAS	9	_____
A STATE OF BEING (EXAMPLE: HAPPINESS, ANGER, CONFUSION, ETC.)	10	_____
AN ITEM YOU MIGHT FIND IN LAS VEGAS	11	_____
ANOTHER STATE OF BEING	12	_____
ANOTHER ITEM YOU MIGHT FIND IN LAS VEGAS	13	_____
SLANG FOR "HUGE"	14	_____

Who can be in doubt of what followed? When any two young

1_____ take it into their heads to marry, they are pretty

sure by 2_____ to carry their point, be they ever so

3_____, or ever so 4_____, or ever so little

likely to be 5_____ to each other's 6_____.

This may be bad 7_____ to conclude with, but I believe it

to be truth; and if such parties succeed, how should 8_____

and 9_____, with the advantage of 10_____

of 11_____, 12_____ of 13_____,

and one 14_____ fortune between them, fail of bearing

down every opposition?

UGLY
LOVE

Every so often, you run into two people who are perfect together. They adore each other, they finish each other's sentences, and they are clearly head over heels in love with each other. You see them together, so in love, and you think to yourself, "How in the world do you spend time with each other without putting paper bags over your heads?" Retool this passage from *Persuasion* to witness a love that, for the good of us all, ought to be blind.

UNFLATTERING ADJECTIVE	1	_____
AN UNFLATTERING PHYSICAL FEATURE	2	_____
ANOTHER UNFLATTERING PHYSICAL FEATURE	3	_____
ANOTHER UNFLATTERING PHYSICAL FEATURE	4	_____
UNFLATTERING ADJECTIVE	5	_____
AN UNFLATTERING PHYSICAL FEATURE	6	_____
ANOTHER UNFLATTERING PHYSICAL FEATURE	7	_____
ANOTHER UNFLATTERING PHYSICAL FEATURE	8	_____
A SKIN CONDITION	9	_____
ADJECTIVE	10	_____
NOUN (PLURAL)	11	_____
ADVERB	12	_____

He was, at that time, a remarkably 1_____ young man, with a great deal of 2_____, 3_____, and 4_____; and Anne an extremely 5_____ girl, with 6_____, 7_____, 8_____, and 9_____. Half the sum of attraction, on either side, might have been enough, for he had nothing to do, and she had hardly anybody to love; but the encounter of such 10_____ 11_____ could not fail. They were gradually acquainted, and when acquainted, 12_____ and deeply in love. It would be difficult to say which had seen highest perfection in the other, or which had been the happiest; she, in receiving his declarations and proposals, or he in having them accepted.

I WOULDN'T
TAKE THAT JOB
IF YOU PAID ME

Anne's father in *Persuasion* notes that sailors "grow older sooner than any other man" because of the salt and sun on their face. Now, that may be, but I've known some pretty grizzled folks of other professions too. I've seen sunken-eyed accountants, haggard restaurant managers, and leathery-skinned new media consultants who fit the bill for having been ridden hard and put away wet. Fill in the blanks to see how your favorite profession does under the effects of hard living.

SOMEONE WHO WORKS IN A TOUGH PROFESSION **1** _____

A FAMILY MEMBER
(EXAMPLE: MOTHER, BROTHER, ETC.) **2** _____

THE PERSON FROM #1'S TOUGH PROFESSION **3** _____

AN ITEM USED IN THIS PROFESSION **4** _____

VERB ASSOCIATED WITH THIS PROFESSION **5** _____

THE PERSON FROM #1 **6** _____

SOMEONE ELSE IN THIS PROFESSION **7** _____

UNAPPEALING NOUN **8** _____

A NUMBER **9** _____

SLANG FOR "A LITTLE" **10** _____

A MARK OF AGE THAT YOU DON'T WANT **11** _____

THE PERSON FROM #7 **12** _____

POSSESSIVE OF THE PROFESSION FROM #3
(EXAMPLE: FIREFIGHTER'S) **13** _____

AN ITEM IN THIS PROFESSION **14** _____

ANOTHER ITEM IN THIS PROFESSION **15** _____

". . . One day last spring, in town, I was in company with two men, striking instances of what I am talking of: **1**_____, whose **2**_____ we all know to have been a **3**_____, without **4**_____ to **5**_____; I was to give place to **6**_____, and a certain **7**_____, the most deplorable-looking personage you can imagine, his face the color of **8**_____, rough and rugged to the last degree, all lines and wrinkles, **9**_____ grey hairs of a side, and nothing but a **10**_____ of **11**_____ at top. . . . I shall not easily forget **12**_____. I never saw quite so wretched an example of what a[n] **13**_____ life can do; but to a degree, I know it is the same with them all: they are all knocked about, and exposed to every **14**_____, and every **15**_____, till they are not fit to be seen. . . ."

CAPTAIN HARVILLE'S
HOME FOR ADVENTUROUS RETIREES

I n *Persuasion*, Captain Harville becomes way busier in his forced retirement than he ever seemed to be in his working life. He sounds a lot like my aunt Fran, who six months into her "relaxing and low-key" retirement took up racquetball, scrapbooking, eavesdropping on the neighbors next door, scuba diving, and basset hound breeding. Fill in the blanks to see how Captain Harville is spending his golden years.

SOMEONE ENGAGED IN A RECREATIONAL ACTIVITY (EXAMPLE: SWIMMER, CHESS PLAYER, MOUNTAIN CLIMBER, ETC.)	1	_____
AN ITEM RELATED TO THE PERSON FROM #1'S ACTIVITY (PLURAL)	2	_____
SOMETHING THAT HOLDS ITEMS (PLURAL)	3	_____
VERB (PAST TENSE)	4	_____
NOUN (PLURAL)	5	_____
A PERSON	6	_____
A STATE OF BEING (EXAMPLE: HAPPINESS, CONFUSION, OLD AGE, ETC.)	7	_____
A FOOD, DRINK, OR DRUG	8	_____
SOMETHING YOU THINK ABOUT	9	_____
SOMETHING ELSE YOU THINK ABOUT	10	_____
VERB (PAST TENSE)	11	_____
VERB (PAST TENSE)	12	_____
VERB (PAST TENSE)	13	_____
VERB (PAST TENSE)	14	_____
NOUN (PLURAL)	15	_____
A GROUP OF PEOPLE (PLURAL)	16	_____
NOUN (PLURAL)	17	_____
NOUN (PLURAL)	18	_____
NOUN	19	_____

Captain Harville was no 1_____; but he had contrived

excellent 2_____, and fashioned very pretty

3_____, for a tolerable collection of well-

4_____ 5_____, the property of

6_____. His 7_____ prevented him from

taking much 8_____; but a mind of 9_____

and 10_____ seemed to furnish him with constant employ-

ment within. He 11_____, he 12_____, he

13_____; he 14_____; he made

15_____ for 16_____, he fashioned new

17_____ and 18_____ with improvements;

and if every thing else was done, sat down to his large

19_____ at one corner of the room.

CAPTAIN BENWICK:
PITCHFORK CONTRIBUTOR

I n *Persuasion*, Anne is forced to spend an evening with Captain Benwick, who is way too into poetry. He's the kind of guy who would read you a sappy sonnet and stare into your eyes with his lip quivering as he said the final line. He probably wouldn't stop quivering until you either acknowledged the genius of the poem or slapped him in the face. Luckily for us, there aren't too many poetry connoisseurs around these days. Unluckily for us, their modern equivalents, hipster indie-music snobs, are still roaming house parties. Fill in the blanks to see what bands Captain Bernwick thinks are great and which bands are "just trying to be Morrissey."

SLANG OR SYNONYM FOR "MUSIC"	1	_____
AN ESOTERIC GENRE OF ROCK	2	_____
A HIPSTER ROCK STAR	3	_____
AN INDIE BAND	4	_____
ANOTHER INDIE BAND	5	_____
ANOTHER INDIE BAND	6	_____
ANOTHER INDIE BAND	7	_____
AN INDIE SONG	8	_____
ANOTHER INDIE SONG	9	_____
A STRANGELY NAMED BAND	10	_____
ANOTHER INDIE BAND	11	_____
THE BAND FROM #10	12	_____
ANOTHER INDIE BAND	13	_____
AN OBSCURE GENRE OF ROCK	14	_____
A TYPICAL HIPSTER SITUATION	15	_____
SOMETHING HIPSTERS LIKE	16	_____
A MUSIC MAGAZINE	17	_____

He was evidently a young man of considerable taste in

1_____, though principally in 2_____. . . .

For, though shy, he did not seem reserved: it had rather the appearance of

3_____; and having talked of 4_____, the

richness of 5_____, and gone through a brief comparison

of 6_____ as to 7_____, trying to ascertain

whether 8_____ or 9_____ were to be

preferred, and how ranked 10_____ and

11_____; and moreover, how 12_____ was to

be pronounced, he showed himself so intimately acquainted with all the

tenderest songs of 13_____, and all the impassioned

descriptions of 14_____; he repeated, with such tremulous

feeling, the various lines which imaged a 15_____, or a

mind destroyed by 16_____, and looked so entirely as if he

meant to be understood, that she ventured to hope he did not always

read 17_____. . . .

From *Pride and Prejudice*

IT IS A TRUTH UNIVERSALLY ACKNOWLEDGED, that a single man in possession of a good fortune must be in want of a wife.

However little known the feelings or views of such a man may be on his first entering a neighborhood, this truth is so well fixed in the minds of the surrounding families, that he is considered as the rightful property of some one or other of their daughters.

"THEN," OBSERVED ELIZABETH, "you must comprehend a great deal in your idea of an accomplished woman."

"Yes; I do comprehend a great deal in it."

"Oh! certainly," cried his faithful assistant, "no one can be really esteemed accomplished, who does not greatly surpass what is usually met with. A woman must have a thorough knowledge of music, singing, drawing, dancing, and the modern languages, to deserve the word; and besides all this, she must possess a certain something in her air and manner of walking, the tone of her voice, her address and expressions, or the word will be but half deserved."

"All this she must possess," added Darcy, "and to all this she must yet add something more substantial, in the improvement of her mind by extensive reading.

WHEN JANE AND ELIZABETH WERE ALONE, the former, who had been cautious in her praise of Mr. Bingley before, expressed to her sister how very much she admired him.

"He is just what a young man ought to be," said she, "sensible, good humored, lively; and I never saw such happy manners!—so much ease, with such perfect good breeding!"

"He is also handsome," replied Elizabeth, "which a young man ought likewise to be, if he possibly can. His character is thereby complete."

"I was very much flattered by his asking me to dance a second time. I did not expect such a compliment."

"WELL," SAID CHARLOTTE, "I wish Jane success with all my heart; and if she were married to him to-morrow, I should think she had as good a chance of happiness as if she were to be studying his character for a twelvemonth. Happiness in marriage is entirely a matter of chance. If the dispositions of the parties are ever so well known to each other, or ever so similar before-hand, it does not advance their felicity in the least. They always contrive to grow sufficiently unlike afterwards to have their share of vexation; and it is better to know as little as possible of the defects of the person with whom you are to pass your life."

"IF MR. DARCY IS NEITHER BY HONOR nor inclination confined to his cousin, why is not he to make another choice? And if I am that choice, why may not I accept him?"

"Because honor, decorum, prudence, nay, interest, forbid it. Yes, Miss Bennet, interest; for do not expect to be noticed by his family or friends, if you willfully act against the inclinations of all. You will be censured, slighted, and despised, by every one connected with him."

HE WAS DECLARED TO BE IN DEBT to every tradesman in the place, and his intrigues, all honored with the title of seduction, had been extended into every tradesman's family. Every body declared that he was the wickedest young man in the world; and every body began to find out that they had always distrusted the appearance of his goodness. Elizabeth, though she did not credit above half of what was said, believed enough to make her former assurance of her sister's ruin still more certain; and even Jane, who believed still less of it, became almost hopeless, more especially as the time was now come when, if they had gone to Scotland, which she had never before entirely despaired of, they must in all probability have gained some news of them.

"IN VAIN HAVE I STRUGGLED. It will not do. My feelings will not be repressed. You must allow me to tell you how ardently I admire and love you."

Elizabeth's astonishment was beyond expression. She stared, colored, doubted, and was silent. This he considered sufficient encouragement, and the avowal of all that he felt and had long felt for her immediately followed. He spoke well, but there were feelings besides those of the heart to be detailed, and he was not more eloquent on the subject of tenderness than of pride.

MR. COLLINS WAS NOT A SENSIBLE MAN, and the deficiency of nature had been but little assisted by education or society; the greatest part of his life having been spent under the guidance of an illiterate and miserly father; and though he belonged to one of the universities, he had merely kept the necessary terms, without forming at it any useful acquaintance. The subjection in which his father had brought him up had given him originally great humility of manner, but it was now a good deal counteracted by the self-conceit of a weak head, living in retirement, and the consequential feelings of early and unexpected prosperity.

From Mansfield Park

FANNY'S IMAGINATION HAD PREPARED HER for something grander than a mere spacious, oblong room, fitted up for the purpose of devotion—with nothing more striking or more solemn than the profusion of mahogany, and the crimson velvet cushions appearing over the ledge of the family gallery above. "I am disappointed," said she, in a low voice to Edmund. "This is not my idea of a chapel. There is nothing awful here, nothing melancholy, nothing grand. Here are no aisles, no arches, no inscriptions, no banners. No banners, cousin, to be 'blown by the night wind of heaven.' No signs that a 'Scottish monarch sleeps below.' "

CRUELTY, DO YOU CALL IT? We differ there. No, hers is not a cruel nature. I do not consider her as meaning to wound my feelings. The evil lies yet deeper: in her total ignorance, unsuspiciousness of there being such feelings; in a perversion of mind which made it natural to her to treat the subject as she did. She was speaking only as she had been used to hear others speak, as she imagined everybody else would speak. Hers are not faults of temper. She would not voluntarily give unnecessary pain to any one, and though I may deceive myself, I cannot but think that for me, for my feelings, she would— Hers are faults of principle, Fanny; of blunted delicacy and a corrupted, vitiated mind.

SHE WAS FEELING, THINKING, TREMBLING about everything; agitated, happy, miserable, infinitely obliged, absolutely angry. It was all beyond belief! He was inexcusable, incomprehensible! But such were his habits that he could do nothing without a mixture of evil. He had previously made her the happiest of human beings, and now he had insulted—she knew not what to say, how to class, or how to regard it. She would not have him be serious, and yet what could excuse the use of such words and offers, if they meant but to trifle?

"I HAD THOUGHT YOU PECULIARLY FREE from willfulness of temper, self-conceit, and every tendency to that independence of spirit which prevails so much in modern days, even in young women, and which in young women is offensive and disgusting beyond all common offense. But you have now shewn me that you can be willful and perverse; that you can and will decide for yourself, without any consideration or deference for those who have surely some right to guide you—without even asking for their advice. You have shewn yourself very, very different from any thing that I had imagined."

FANNY READ TO HERSELF THAT "it was with infinite concern the newspaper had to announce to the world a matrimonial *fracas* in the family of Mr. R. of Wimpole Street; the beautiful Mrs. R., whose name had not long been enrolled in the lists of Hymen, and who had promised to become so brilliant a leader in the fashionable world, having quitted her husband's roof in company with the well-known and captivating Mr. C., the intimate friend and associate of Mr. R., and it was not known even to the editor of the newspaper whither they were gone."

"WHAT! TAKE ORDERS WITHOUT A LIVING?! No, that is madness indeed; absolute madness."

"Shall I ask you how the church is to be filled, if a man is neither to take orders with a living, nor without?. . . As he cannot be influenced by those feeling's which you rank highly as temptation and reward to the soldier and sailor, in their choice of a profession, as heroism, and noise, and fashion, are all against him . . . "

"Oh!, no doubt he is very sincere in preferring an income ready made, to the trouble of working for one; and has the best intentions of doing nothing all the rest of his days but eat, drink, and grow fat. . . . A clergyman has nothing to do but be slovenly and selfish—read the newspaper, watch the weather, and quarrel with his wife. His curate does all the work, and the business of his own life is to dine."

From *Emma*

EMMA WOODHOUSE, HANDSOME, CLEVER, AND RICH, with a comfortable home and happy disposition, seemed to unite some of the best blessings of existence; and had lived nearly twenty-one years in the world with very little to distress or vex her. . . .

The real evils, indeed, of Emma's situation were the power of having rather too much her own way, and a disposition to think a little too well of herself; these were the disadvantages which threatened alloy to her many enjoyments. The danger, however, was at the present so unperceived, that they did not by any means rank as misfortunes with her.

"NEVER MIND, HARRIET, I SHALL NOT BE a poor old maid; and it is poverty only which makes celibacy contemptible to a generous public! A single woman, with a very narrow income, must be a ridiculous, disagreeable old maid! the proper sport of boys and girls; but a single woman, of good fortune, is always respectable, and may be as sensible and pleasant as anybody else. And the distinction is not quite so much against the candor and common sense of the world as appears at first; for a very narrow income has a tendency to contract the mind, and sour the temper. Those who can barely live, and who live perforce in a very small, and generally very inferior, society, may well be illiberal and cross. This does not apply, however, to Miss Bates; she is only too good natured and too silly to suit me; but, in general, she is very much to the taste of everybody, though single and though poor."

MRS. COLE WAS TELLING THAT SHE had been calling on Miss Bates, and as soon as she entered the room had been struck by the sight of a pianoforte—a very elegant-looking instrument—not a grand, but a large-sized square pianoforte; and the substance of the story, the end of all the dialogue which ensued of surprise, and inquiry, and congratulations on her side, and explanations on Miss Bates's, was, that this pianoforte had arrived from Broadwood's the day before, to the great astonishment of both aunt and niece—entirely unexpected; that at first, by Miss Bates's account, Jane herself was quite at a loss, quite bewildered to think who could possibly have ordered it—but now, they were both perfectly satisfied that it could be from only one quarter;—of course it must be from Colonel Campbell.

ABOUT HALF A MILE BEYOND HIGHBURY, making a sudden turn, and deeply shaded by elms on each side, it became for a considerable stretch very retired; and when the young ladies had advanced some way into it, they had suddenly perceived, at a small distance before them...a party of gypsies. A child on the watch came towards them to beg; and Miss Bickerton, excessively frightened, gave a great scream, and calling on Harriet to follow her, ran up a steep bank, cleared a slight hedge at the top, and made the best of her way by a short cut back to Highbury. But poor Harriet could not follow. . . .

Harriet was soon assailed by half a dozen children, headed by a stout woman and a great boy, all clamorous, and impertinent in look, though not absolutely in word. More and more frightened, she immediately promised them money, and taking out her purse, gave them a shilling, and begged them not to want more, or to use her ill. She was then able to walk, though but slowly, and was moving away—but her terror and her purse were too tempting, and she was followed, or rather surrounded, by the whole gang, demanding more.

"NOT HARRIET'S EQUAL!" exclaimed Mr. Knightley loudly and warmly; and with calmer asperity, added, a few moments afterwards, "No, he is not her equal indeed, for he is as much her superior in sense as in situation. Emma, your infatuation about that girl blinds you. What are Harriet Smith's claims, either of birth, nature or education, to any connection higher than Robert Martin? She is the natural daughter of nobody knows whom, with probably no settled provision at all, and certainly no respectable relations. She is known only as parlor-boarder at a common school. She is not a sensible girl, nor a girl of any information. She has been taught nothing useful, and is too young and too simple to have acquired any thing herself. At her age she can have no experience, and with her little wit, is not very likely ever to have any that can avail her. She is pretty, and she is good tempered, and that is all."

BUT NOW, SHE WOULD RATHER IT HAD NOT HAPPENED. She believed he had been drinking too much of Mr. Weston's good wine, and felt sure that he would want to be talking nonsense.

To restrain him as much as might be, by her own manners, she was immediately preparing to speak with exquisite calmness and gravity of the weather and the night; but scarcely had she begun, scarcely had they passed the sweep-gate and joined the other carriage, than she found her subject cut up—her hand seized—her attention demanded, and Mr. Elton actually making violent love to her: availing himself of the precious opportunity, declaring sentiments which must be already well known, hoping—fearing—adoring—ready to die if she refused him; but flattering himself that his ardent attachment and unequaled love and unexampled passion could not fail of having some effect, and in short, very much resolved on being seriously accepted as soon as possible. It really was so. . . . She felt that half this folly must be drunkenness, and therefore could hope that it might belong only to the passing hour.

"AND HOW DID YOU THINK MISS FAIRFAX LOOKING?"

"Ill, very ill—that is, if a young lady can ever be allowed to look ill. But the expression is hardly admissible, Mrs. Weston, is it? Ladies can never look ill. And, seriously, Miss Fairfax is naturally so pale, as almost always to give the appearance of ill health.—A most deplorable want of complexion."

Emma would not agree to this, and began a warm defense of Miss Fairfax's complexion. "It was certainly never brilliant, but she would not allow it to have a sickly hue in general; and there was a softness and delicacy in her skin which gave peculiar elegance to the character of her face." He listened with all due deference; acknowledged that he had heard many people say the same—but yet he must confess, that to him nothing could make amends for the want of the fine glow of health.

From *Sense and Sensibility*

"OF HIS SENSE AND HIS GOODNESS," continued Elinor, "no one can, I think, be in doubt, who has seen him often enough to engage him in unreserved conversation. The excellence of his understanding and his principles can be concealed only by that shyness which too often keeps him silent. You know enough of him to do justice to his solid worth. . . . I have seen a great deal of him, have studied his sentiments, and heard his opinion on subjects of literature and taste; and, upon the whole, I venture to pronounce that his mind is well-informed, his enjoyment of books exceedingly great, his imagination lively, his observation just and correct, and his taste delicate and pure. His abilities in every respect improve as much upon acquaintance as his manners and person. At first sight, his address is certainly not striking; and his person can hardly be called handsome, till the expression of his eyes, which are uncommonly good, and the general sweetness of his countenance, is perceived. At present, I know him so well, that I think him really handsome; or, at least, almost so. What say you, Marianne?"

"I SHALL VERY SOON THINK HIM HANDSOME, Elinor, if I do not now. When you tell me to love him as a brother, I shall no more see imperfection in his face than I now do in his heart."

Elinor started at this declaration, and was sorry for the warmth she had been betrayed into in speaking of him. She felt that Edward stood very high in her opinion. She believed the regard to be mutual; but she required greater certainty of it to make Marianne's conviction of their attachment agreeable to her. . . . "I do not attempt to deny," said she, "that I think very highly of him— that I greatly esteem, that I like him."

Marianne here burst forth with indignation—"Esteem him! Like him! Cold-hearted Elinor! Oh! worse than cold-hearted! Ashamed of being otherwise. Use those words again, and I will leave the room this moment."

THE GENTLEMAN OFFERED HIS SERVICES; and perceiving that her modesty declined what her situation rendered necessary, took her up in his arms, without farther delay, and carried her down the hill. . . .

His manly beauty and more than common gracefulness were instantly the theme of general admiration; and the laugh which his gallantry raised against Marianne received particular spirit from his exterior attractions. Marianne herself had seen less of his person than the rest, for the confusion which crimsoned over her face, on his lifting her up, had robbed her of the power of regarding him after their entering the house. But she had seen enough of him to join in all the admiration of the others, and with an energy which always adorned her praise. His person and air were equal to what her fancy had ever drawn for the hero of a favorite story; and in his carrying her into the house with so little previous formality there was a rapidity of thought which particularly recommended the action to her. Every circumstance belonging to him was interesting. His name was good, his residence was in their favorite village, and she soon found out that of all manly dresses a shooting-jacket was the most becoming.

BUT ELINOR—HOW ARE HER FEELINGS to be described? From the moment of learning that Lucy was married to another, that Edward was free, to the moment of his justifying the hopes which had so instantly followed, she was every thing by turns but tranquil. But when the second moment had passed, when she found every doubt, every solicitude removed, compared her situation with what so lately it had been,—saw him honorably released from his former engagement—saw him instantly profiting by the release, to address herself and declare an affection as tender, as constant as she had ever supposed it to be,—

she was oppressed, she was overcome by her own felicity; and happily disposed as is the human mind to be easily familiarized with any change for the better, it required several hours to give sedateness to her spirits, or any degree of tranquility to her heart.

"STRANGE IF IT WOULD!" cried Marianne. "What have wealth or grandeur to do with happiness?"

"Grandeur has but little," said Elinor, "but wealth has much to do with it."

"Elinor, for shame!" said Marianne; "money can only give happiness where there is nothing else to give it. Beyond a competence, it can afford no real satisfaction, as far as mere self is concerned."

"Perhaps," said Elinor, smiling, "we may come to the same point. *Your* competence and *my* wealth are very much alike, I dare say…Come, what is your competence?"

"About eighteen hundred or two thousand a year; not more than *that*." Elinor laughed. "*Two* thousand a year! *One* is my wealth! I guessed how it would end."

"And yet two thousand a year is a very moderate income," said Marianne. "A family cannot well be maintained on a smaller. I am sure I am not extravagant in my demands. A proper establishment of servants, a carriage, perhaps two, and hunters, cannot be supported on less."

WHEN THEIR PROMISED VISIT TO THE PARK, and consequent introduction to these young ladies, took place, they found in the appearance of the eldest, who was nearly thirty, with a very plain and not a sensible face, nothing to admire; but in the other, who, was not more than two or three and twenty, they acknowledged considerable beauty: her features were pretty, and she had a sharp quick eye, and a smartness of air, which though it did not give actual elegance or grace, gave distinction to her person. Their manners were particularly civil, and Elinor soon allowed them credit for some kind of sense, when she saw with what constant and judicious attention they were making themselves agreeable to Lady Middleton. With her children they were in continual raptures, extolling their beauty, courting their notice, and humoring all their whims; and such of their time as could be spared from the importunate demands which this politeness made on it, was spent in admiration of whatever her ladyship was doing, if she happened to be doing any thing, or in taking patterns of some elegant new dress, in which her appearance the day before had thrown them into unceasing delight.

MRS. JENNINGS, LADY MIDDLETON'S MOTHER, was a good-humored, merry, fat, elderly woman, who talked a great deal, seemed very happy, and rather vulgar. She was full of jokes and laughter, and before dinner was over had said many witty things on the subject of lovers and husbands; hoped they had not left their hearts behind them in Sussex, and pretended to see them blush whether they did or not. Marianne was vexed at it for her sister's sake, and turned her eyes towards Elinor to see how she bore these attacks, with an earnestness which gave Elinor far more pain than could arise from such common-place raillery as Mrs. Jennings's.

From *Northanger Abby*

NORTHANGER ABBEY! These were thrilling words, and wound up Catherine's feelings to the highest point of ecstasy. Her grateful and gratified heart could hardly restrain its expressions within the language of tolerable calmness. To receive so flattering an invitation! To have her company so warmly solicited! Everything honorable and soothing, every present enjoyment, and every future hope was contained in it; and her acceptance, with only the saving clause of Papa and Mamma's approbation, was eagerly given. "I will write home directly," said she, "and if they do not object, as I dare say they will not—"

"IF I UNDERSTAND YOU RIGHTLY, you had formed a surmise of such horror as I have hardly words to—Dear Miss Morland, consider the dreadful nature of the suspicions you have entertained. What have you been judging from? Remember the country and the age in which we live. Remember that we are English, that we are Christians. Consult your own understanding, your own sense of the probable, your own observation of what is passing around you. Does our education prepare us for such atrocities? Do our laws connive at them? Could they be perpetrated without being known, in a country like this, where social and literary intercourse is on such a footing; where every man is surrounded by a neighborhood of voluntary spies; and where roads and newspapers lay everything open?"

SHE PAUSED A MOMENT IN BREATHLESS WONDER. The wind roared down the chimney, the rain beat in torrents against the windows, and everything seemed to speak the awfulness of her situation. To retire to bed, however, unsatisfied on such a point, would be vain, since sleep must be impossible with the consciousness of a cabinet so mysteriously closed in her immediate vicinity. Again, therefore, she applied herself to the key, and after moving it in every possible way for some instants, with the determined celerity of hope's last effort, the door suddenly yielded to her hand.

"OH!, NO, I ONLY MEAN WHAT I have read about. It always puts me in mind of the country that Emily and her father traveled through, in *The Mysteries of Udolpho*. But you never read novels, I dare say?"

"Why not?"

"Because they are not clever enough for you—gentlemen read better books."

"The person, be it gentleman or lady, who has not pleasure in a good novel, must be intolerably stupid. I have read all Mrs. Radcliffe's works, and most of them with great pleasure. *The Mysteries of Udolpho*, when I had once begun it, I could not lay down again; I remember finishing it in two days—my hair standing on end the whole time."

"Yes," added Miss Tilney, "and I remember that you undertook to read it aloud to me, and that when I was called away for only five minutes to answer a note, instead of waiting for me, you took the volume into the Hermitage Walk, and I was obliged to stay till you had finished it."

"HISTORIANS, YOU THINK," said Miss Tilney, "are not happy in their flights of fancy. They display imagination without raising interest. I am fond of history and am very well contented to take the false with the true. In the principal facts they have sources of intelligence in former histories and records, which may be as much depended on, I conclude, as anything that does not actually pass under one's own observation; and as for the little embellishments you speak of, they are embellishments, and I like them as such. If a speech be well drawn up, I read it with pleasure, by whomsoever it may be made—and probably with much greater, if the production of Mr. Hume or Mr. Robertson, than if the genuine words of Caractacus, Agricola, or Alfred the Great."

"OXFORD! THERE IS NO DRINKING AT OXFORD NOW, I assure you. Nobody drinks there. You would hardly meet with a man who goes beyond his four pints at the utmost. Now, for instance, it was reckoned a remarkable thing at the last party in my rooms, that upon an average we cleared about five pints a head. It was looked upon as something out of the common way. *Mine* is famous good stuff, to be sure. You would not often meet with anything like it in Oxford.

From *Persuasion*

ANNE'S MIND WAS IN A MOST FAVORABLE STATE for the entertainment of the evening: it was just occupation enough: she had feelings for the tender, spirits for the gay, attention for the scientific, and patience for the wearisome; and had never liked a concert better, at least during the first act. Towards the close of it, in the interval succeeding an Italian song, she explained the words of the song to Mr. Elliot. They had a concert bill between them.

WHO CAN BE IN DOUBT OF WHAT FOLLOWED? When any two young people take it into their heads to marry, they are pretty sure by perseverance to carry their point, be they ever so poor, or ever so imprudent, or ever so little likely to be necessary to each other's ultimate comfort. This may be bad morality to conclude with, but I believe it to be truth; and if such parties succeed, how should a Captain Wentworth and an Anne Elliot, with the advantage of maturity of mind, consciousness of right, and one independent fortune between them, fail of bearing down every opposition?

HE WAS, AT THAT TIME, a remarkably fine young man, with a great deal of intelligence, spirit, and brilliancy; and Anne an extremely pretty girl, with gentleness, modesty, taste, and feeling. Half the sum of attraction, on either side, might have been enough, for he had nothing to do, and she had hardly anybody to love; but the encounter of such lavish recommendations could not fail. They were gradually acquainted, and when acquainted, rapidly and deeply in love. It would be difficult to say which had seen highest perfection in the other, or which had been the happiest; she, in receiving his declarations and proposals, or he in having them accepted.

"... **ONE DAY LAST SPRING,** in town, I was in company with two men, striking instances of what I am talking of: Lord St. Ives, whose father we all know to have been a country curate, without bread to eat; I was to give place to Lord St. Ives, and a certain Admiral Baldwin, the most-deplorable looking personage you can imagine, his face the color of mahogany, rough and rugged to the last degree, all lines and wrinkles, nine grey hairs of a side, and nothing but a dab of powder at top. . . . I shall not easily forget Admiral Baldwin. I never saw quite so wretched an example of what a sea-faring life can do; but to a degree, I know it is the same with them all: they are all knocked about, and exposed to every climate, and every weather, till they are not fit to be seen. . . ."

CAPTAIN HARVILLE WAS NO READER; but he had contrived excellent accommodations, and fashioned very pretty shelves, for a tolerable collection of well-bound volumes, the property of Captain Benwick. His lameness prevented him from taking much exercise; but a mind of usefulness and ingenuity seemed to furnish him with constant employment within. He drew, he varnished, he carpentered, he glued; he made toys for the children; he fashioned new netting-needles and pins with improvements; and if every thing else was done, sat down to his large fishing-net at one corner of the room.

HE WAS EVIDENTLY A YOUNG MAN of considerable taste in reading, though principally in poetry. . . For, though shy, he did not seem reserved: it had rather the appearance of feelings glad to burst their usual restraints; and having talked of poetry, the richness of the present age, and gone through a brief comparison of opinion as to the first-rate poets, trying to ascertain whether *Marmion* or *The Lady of the Lake* were to be preferred, and how ranked the *Giaour* and *The Bride of Abydos*; and moreover, how the *Giaour* was to be pronounced, he showed himself so intimately acquainted with all the tenderest songs of the one poet, and all the impassioned descriptions of hopeless agony of the other; he repeated, with such tremulous feeling, the various lines which imaged a broken heart, or a mind destroyed by wretchedness, and looked so entirely as if he meant to be understood, that she ventured to hope he did not always read only poetry . . .